Fast Bytes

Perfect Scanning

M. Gradias

DATA BECKER®

Copyright © 2001 by   DATA BECKER GmbH & Co. KG
                       Merowingerstr. 30
                       40223 Düsseldorf

Copyright © 2002 by   DATA BECKER CORP
                       154 Wells Avenue
                       Newton
                       MA 02459

Published by   DATA BECKER CORP
                       154 Wells Avenue
                       Newton
                       MA 02459

Author   Michael Gradias

Printed in the United States   May 2002

UPC CODE   6-80466-90210-2

ISBN #   1-58507-115-3

DATABECKER® is a registered trademark no. 2 017 966

Contents

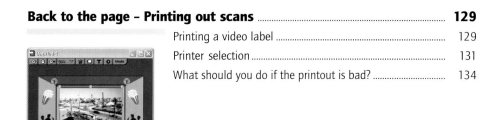

Introduction

You just bought a new scanner? Maybe it's one of those bargain buys available everywhere? Do you want to know how to best use your new toy?

Then this book is perfect for you. It teaches you everything you ever need to know about scanning. It's amazing what you can do with a scanner! Learn how to install your new acquisition and which options your new scanner software is offering you.

By means of many practical examples, I show you how to obtain acceptable images from low-quality ones, as well as how to apply different effects to enhance your pictures.

Have fun with this book and your new scanner!

Michael Gradias

Let's get started: The first scan

Before you can scan your first image, you must spend some time on preparing. In this chapter, you look more closely at these steps by providing a brief outline of the preparations.

The third chapter describes the individual steps in detail.

Releasing the transport lock

Many scanners contain a transport lock to make sure that the scanning unit is not damaged during transportation. You should check if the transportation lock is mentioned either on the scanner itself or in your scanner manual.

It is essential that you release the transportation lock before starting to scan, as your scanner might be damaged otherwise.

Plugging in your scanner

Once you have set up your scanner, you must first – you guessed it – plug it in.

1 Use the provided power cable to connect your scanner to the power supply. Then connect the scanner to your computer.

2 The scanner might be plugged into your computer's printer port, or you can hook it up as a SCSI device – depending on your scanner model. Or you might also use a modern USB connection, as shown in the illustration.

Different ways of connecting your scanner

Scanners are available for three different kinds of connections – they can be connected to your PC through the printer port (LPT), a USB device, or a SCSI interface.

3 If you want to connect your scanner to the LPT interface, the printer cable must be plugged into the back of your scanner; otherwise, you cannot print anymore. In computer lingo, this is called looping through.

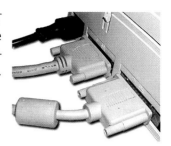

My printer doesn't work anymore!

Some scanner models only allow you to print if the scanner is turned on. This might be inconvenient, but you have to live with it – especially if you bought a scanner at the low end of the price scale.

Connecting through the USB interface

USB (**U**niversal **S**erial **B**us) is a new bus system that can be used to connect different terminal devices such as the mouse, the printer, or the scanner. This way you can Plug and Play. As with LPT interfaces, you don't need to turn on your computer.

USB devices also have the advantage of not having their own power cable; therefore, you don't need an additional power supply. An increasing number of terminal devices are equipped with this kind of connection. Because of the Plug and Play capability, it is not necessary to reboot the computer. Simply connect the scanner to the USB interface; then go to the *Device Manger* to update your system. You can now access your scanner by means of your scanner driver.

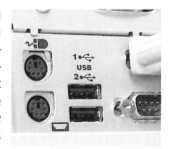

Windows 95 and NT do not support USB

You need Windows 98 or higher to use USB interfaces due to driver availability.

The system is updated

If you are using a Plug and Play scanner, Windows should automatically recognize the added device.

If this is not the case, you must manually update your system. The following steps are required:

1 Open the Control Panel through the Windows Start menu.

2 The Control Panel contains the *Add Hardware* icon that is highlighted in the illustration.

3 Click the icon to start the Add Hardware Wizard. This Wizard carries out the required steps.

The process of finding new hardware components might take a little while.

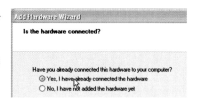

The INF file contains the required driver information

Once your new scanner has been found, you are asked to specify the location of its driver. Please refer to your scanner documentation to find the corresponding INF file containing the required driver information.

12

Up-to-date drivers from the Internet

Is your scanner driver out-of-date? Then check out the following Web sites:

Web address	
www.driverguide.com	many drivers from different manufacturers
www.drivershq.com	links to drivers; also "exotic" ones
http://www.galttech.com/drivers.shtml	offers a huge driver archive
http://totallydrivers.com/	tons of different device drivers

Installing the TWAIN module

You must install the TWAIN module that acts as a go-between between your scanner and image editing software. It is a separate program used to transfer images to your image-editing program.

Your scanner box should therefore also contain software – probably on a CD. Depending on your scanner package, you might even find a number of software CDs. The scanner used in the examples, Epson Perfection 1240U, came with a number of CDs containing lots of different programs. Look for the CD containing the TWAIN driver – usually, it is the first CD. Depending on the scanner model you are using, a different setup program for installing the TWAIN software starts. You might want to refer to your manual to find out more about this procedure.

With the scanner used here, a setup program – which is illustrated – was automatically started once we entered the first CD. The setup program of your scanner might look entirely different, however.

Click the corresponding icon to start the setup program. You are then guided through the installation by means of different dialog boxes; it's really simple and straightforward.

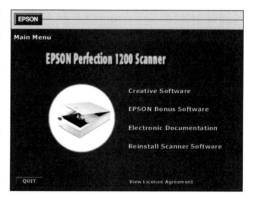

Installing the provided software

All that's left to do is to install the provided software, which is needed for image editing or text recognition, for instance. You learn more about these two areas in the following chapters.

The included programs differ from scanner model to scanner model. Some scanners come with many – even high-end – programs, and others come only with lighter versions of well-known programs such as Corel PHOTO-PAINT or Photoshop. Sometimes, older versions of these well-known (and expensive) programs might be provided with your scanner.

Important software: Image editing programs

To modify images, you need image editing programs. Two well-known examples of this group of programs are Corel PHOTO-PAINT and Micrografx Publisher.

Many scanners come with programs developed by Ulead or Adobe. Ulead manufactures popular image-editing programs such as Photo Impact and Photo Express. Adobe PhotoDeluxe is considered a high-end image-editing program. A version of this program was provided with the scanner used for this book.

In our case, the setup program was started automatically once we inserted the CD. As usual, you are guided through the installation by means of a setup Wizard and different dialog boxes that ask you for the required information.

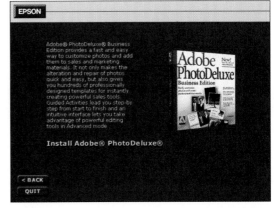

OCR software

If you don't feel like typing in printed text, use OCR programs to turn black-and-white scans into editable text. Unfortunately, many OCR programs provided with scanners have a serious shortcoming. Very often, they are only versions with a highly limited scope of features, and some OCR programs can be used only for a certain period of time.

Additional auxiliary programs

Your scanner might also come with a number of auxiliary programs. Our scanner, for instance, was provided with a Smart Panel to quickly start different auxiliary programs. These programs enable you to e-mail your scans, for instance, or to create copies of them.

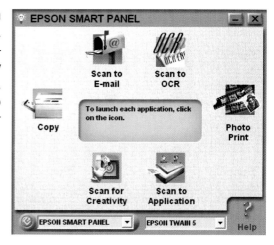

Restarting Windows for your new settings to take effect

Once all programs have been installed, you should restart Windows so that all changes can take effect. This is important, as many programs add different settings to your Windows registry database.

Scanning your first photo

Once you have completed all scanning preparations, you can start scanning. In this chapter, you learn about scanning your first image. In addition, you discover important points to consider.

1. Let's get started: The first scan

Starting the image editing program

To start scanning, you must open the image editing program that was provided with your scanner - and don't worry, it doesn't matter if it's not the one illustrated here.

After opening our sample program, Adobe PhotoDeluxe, the work area appears to be nearly empty - as shown in the illustration below.

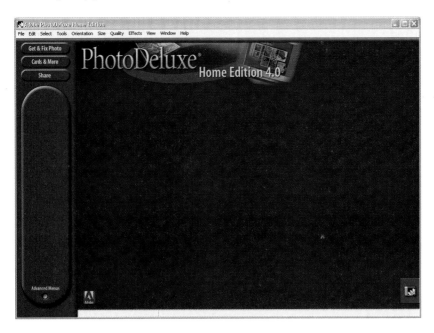

1 The next steps are easy - click *Get & Fix Photo* on the left side ...

2 ... and a toolbar displays at the top of the work area.

3 Click the *Get Photo* icon to open the dialog box illustrated here.

A menu opens from which you can select different options for importing images. Select the *Scanners* option.

4 The toolbar changes. At the very top, three steps are displayed. Select the first step (which is *Scanner*).

5 The *Choose Scanner* icon appears.

6 You must choose the TWAIN module of the scanner you would like to use.

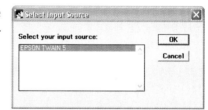

Selecting the correct scanner

If only one TWAIN module is installed on your computer, you should not worry when using an image-editing program. If you have a number of modules installed, however, you must first let the image-editing program know which module to use. This procedure is similar to all image-editing programs – even if the commands differ slightly. Usually, the *File* menu contains the submenu *Import*, from which you can select the command *Select TWAIN 32 source*. This way, the illustrated dialog box opens, from which you can choose the corresponding TWAIN module.

1. Let's get started: The first scan

Additional programs

Some scanners might come with a number of TWAIN modules – there might be a simple version without any fancy program features, as well as a "pro" version with many functions to influence the scanning results.

Scanning with the TWAIN driver

Depending on the type of scanner, the TWAIN module might differ greatly. You start the TWAIN module by clicking *Scan*.

The illustration shows the Epson TWAIN 5 module – many different options are available.

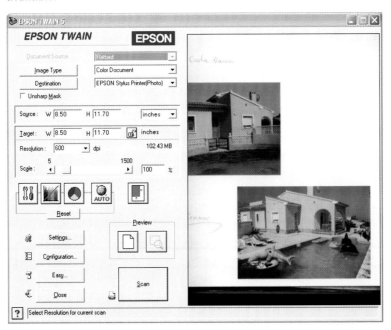

No image without a prescan

Some scanners – such as the Epson model – automatically create a preview scan. If your preview window is empty, choose the *Preview* option. Depending on the TWAIN module you use, this option could have a different name, such as *Prescan*, for instance.

1 During the prescan, the scanner surface is scanned and then displayed in the preview image.

2 The current settings – which can be defined on the left side of the dialog window – are used for the prescan.

Therefore, you might only see a black-and-white image initially, depending on the default settings.

Selecting the correct scan area

If you simply clicked the *Scan* button, the entire scan surface would be scanned, which is entirely unnecessary of course. As the surrounding, bright area is of no use, only the required portion of the scan area should be selected, that is, the area containing the image to be scanned.

1 If you place your mouse pointer over the preview image, a cross-hair symbol appears. Click the top left corner and press your left mouse button.

2 Drag your mouse and draw a frame around the photo to be scanned. The square indicates the area to be scanned.

3 Once you release the mouse button, the frame appears as a broken line, indicating your selection. You can use it to modify the width of your selection.

4 If you place your mouse pointer on top of one edge of the frame, a symbol is displayed, indicating the frame's stretching options. This way you can modify the selection frame later on if desired.

Note

Wrong selection?

Are you wondering why a small white border has been left around your image? Well, this is actually intentional. Unfortunately, there are many TWAIN modules that do not take selection frames very "seriously". Even if you selected the perfect image area, some parts of the image might have been simply cut off in the scanned image. Therefore, it is a good idea to leave a little bit of the border around your image to make sure the entire image is scanned.

Customizing: The correct scan settings

Now that you have defined the area to be scanned, you must also choose the appropriate settings. Again, these settings might differ from one TWAIN module to the next; however, they are usually similar in all TWAIN modules.

1 You can see the available setting options on the left side of the dialog box.

2 The top list box allows you to choose whether a flatbed scanner or a transparency adapter for slides should be used. Naturally, this option is available only if you are actually using a scanner with a transparency adapter.

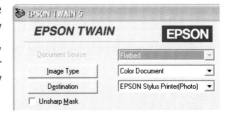

3 The *Image Type* list box allows you to specify whether the image to be scanned is a color or black-and-white image.

Click *Image Type*; a separate dialog box appears displaying the detailed options. Accept the default options for now.

4 The *Destination* list box offers different output devices. Again, if you click the *Destination* button, a separate dialog box opens to display the options in detail.

You can also change the resolution of your scan at this point.

What are output devices?

Are you wondering about output devices? The device that the image uses at the end of the process is called the output device.

If you want to look at your photo on your monitor only, you must select the *Monitor* option. If it should be printed later on, you must choose the corresponding option. PhotoDeluxe bases the scanning resolution on this particular setting.

5 The following text entry fields allow you to specify whether the image should be scanned in its original size or whether you want to change its size.

6 The lower section contains buttons that can be used to optimize the image – if the option *Auto* is selected, the program automatically chooses the best values.

1. Let's get started: The first scan

Ready, steady, go! Starting the scanning process

This particular TWAIN module does not require further information. Therefore, click the *Scan* button to start the scanning process.

Scanning duration

The required scanning time depends on the size of the image to be scanned. The larger the image, the longer it takes to scan the entire image.

Once the image has been entirely scanned, the TWAIN module is not needed anymore – unless you want to scan a number of images at once. If this is not the case, close the TWAIN module by clicking *Close*. Once the TWAIN module has been closed, click the third command displayed in the top toolbar: *Done*. The regular toolbar appears again.

Displaying the image at the right size

PhotoDeluxe automatically chooses the image's display size to ensure that it can be seen in its entirety on the screen.

Trimming images: Cutting off image borders

Because some of the white border around the image was scanned intentionally, you must remove it now. Every image-editing program offers a tool for this purpose. It is usually called the trimming (or cropping) tool.

1 In PhotoDeluxe, you can access this tool by going to *Rotate & Size*. The function you are looking for is called *Trim & Size*.

2 To cut off certain parts of the image, select the first step. The toolbar changes again and displays a different set of functions.

3 Now draw a selection frame around your image as desired. You can also use the handles in the four corners to modify your selection afterwards.

23

4 If you are satisfied with the selection, click *OK* to trim the image.

Optimizing images the fast way

This chapter is not about elaborately optimizing images: the image looks fairly good, even though the automatic settings were used. Nevertheless, it could look even better. This task can be taken care of within a few steps and with a fully automatic function.

1 Go to *Adjust Quality* and select the *Appearance* function.

2 Click the first step and select the function *Instant Fix*.

That's it. The resulting image has more contrast and richer colors.

Saving the fruit of your labor

Now that you have optimized your image, all that's left is to save it on your hard disk. You can find the corresponding function under *Save & Send*. The functions *Save* and *Export* are of interest to you.

Saving that makes sense

If you select the *Save* function, the image is saved in the PhotoDeluxe-specific file format PDD. This format also saves any additional information (if you add text to your image, for instance). If you want to use the image in another program, such as a text-editing program, select the *Export* option. All current file formats that are recognized by other programs are available to you.

1 To save the image in the popular TIF format, go to *Save & Send* and select the *Export* function.

2 Click step *1 Export* and select the option *Other Export*.

3 Select the TIF format from the *Save As* list box of the dialog box that appears and enter the desired file name.

That's it!

The correct resolution and the best-suited color mode

This chapter introduces important scanning basics. You learn about choosing the correct resolution and the best-suited color mode.

Scanning at optimum resolution

Resolution – this term appears over and over again when scanning, and that's exactly why you need to find out why this value is of such great importance.

Dpi, lpi, ppi, interpolated resolution – these are just a few terms that confuse the novice user. Before you decide which resolution is the correct one, learn what the term resolution means.

The resolution value determines the number of pixels in a certain unit of measurement. When you look at the following image, you might be asking, "Well, what are pixels?" The image appears quite "normal", doesn't it? And that's the way it should be. Normally, pixels are so small that you cannot see them individually.

To recognize a pixel, an image has to be highly magnified. The following image shows an enlarged part of the previous one.

You can see many small squares in the enlargement: these are the pixels that make up the image. The first image contains many of these pixels, and they are too small to be recognized.

So what would happen if the image would contain fewer pixels? Let's take a look!

The difference is clearly visible: the image quality is bad. The individual pixels can be recognized with the naked eye, so there's no point in magnifying the image.

What happened?

Well, the width of the first image contained more than 800 pixels, whereas the second one contained about 200.

Let's do some math!

The first image has a width of 7 cm. As the image width contains 826 pixels, 118 pixels appear per centimeter, which can be converted to exactly 300 pixels per inch (that is, 300 dpi).

The second image also has a width of 7 cm – and is only 193 pixels wide. This means there are 27 pixels per cm, which equals 70 dpi.

Professional jargon

Let's talk like the pros: the first image has a resolution of 300 dpi, and the second has a resolution of 70 dpi.

How is this value calculated? Dpi is the abbreviation for dots per inch or pixel per inch. One inch equals 2.54 cm.

The connection between image size and resolution

You have seen from the previous examples that a certain number of pixels per inch are required to obtain good image quality.

The standard resolution for printed products is 300 dpi, which is why the first result looked pretty good. To obtain an acceptable print of the second picture – which was 193 pixels wide – we would have to scale it down considerably. You can see the result opposite.

This image still contains the same number of pixels, but because the image is considerably smaller, the individual pixels are not recognizable anymore.

The optimum screen resolution

You now know about the correct resolution for printing images, but what if you actually don't want to print your picture? Maybe you only want to use it on your screen, for instance, as part of your Web page.

In this case, a number of different considerations must be taken into account. First of all, you should find out the screen resolution of your monitor:

1 Right-click an empty spot of your Windows desktop. A pop-up menu containing the entry *Properties* opens.

2 Click this entry to open the *Display Properties* dialog box.

The *Settings* tab displays the current settings of your graphics card.

3 The *Screen resolution* section allows you to change the screen resolution by using the slider; in this example, the screen resolution is set to 1,024 x 768 pixels.

4 Drag the slider to the left to change the screen resolution; try a resolution of 800 x 600 pixels.

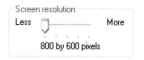

If you look at the images at this screen resolution, notice that the small image takes up approximately a third of the screen width. This makes sense, if you consider that the image is 193 pixels wide and the screen is now 600 pixels wide.

Only parts of the second image are visible, however. Because it is 826 pixels wide, it doesn't fit entirely on the screen.

In addition, notice that all of the toolbars of the image-editing program – in this example Photoshop 6 is used – appear to be rather big. This is why they are partly hidden in the second image; otherwise, you would not see much of the actual image.

2. The correct resolution and the best-suited color mode

You can see both versions in the following illustrations.

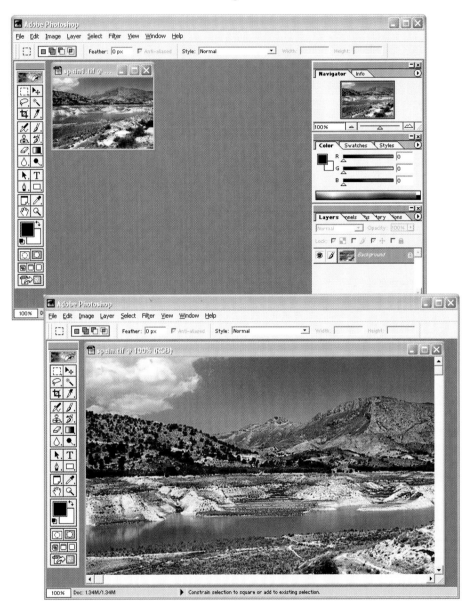

If you set the screen resolution to 1,024 x 768 pixels, the screen looks entirely different. Both images now fit on the screen simultaneously.

The controls, however, appear pretty small right now, as you can see in the following image.

Calculating the screen resolution

The screen resolution can easily be calculated in dpi:

Simply take a ruler and measure the width of your screen. In the case of a 17-inch monitor, the screen width is approximately 12.6 inches. If you use a screen resolution of 1,024 x 768 pixels, one inch contains 81 pixels. This means that your screen resolution is 81 dpi, which is pretty much the standard value for all monitor settings.

2. The correct resolution and the best-suited color mode

How many pixels does your image contain?

You now know that the most important value needed to determine the resolution is the number of pixels. This is why every program displays the image size in pixels.

1 In PhotoDeluxe, click the measurements displayed in the footer of the image window to see the number of pixels.

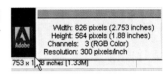

2 Other programs might provide you with tons of information about an image.

In Corel PHOTO-PAINT™ 9, you obtain lots of additional information about an image by going to *File/Document Info* and opening the dialog box illustrated.

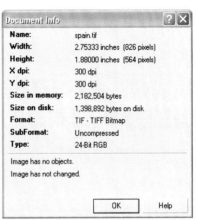

3 If you are using the shareware program Paint Shop Pro 7, go to *Image/Image Information* for details about your image. Apart from the number of pixels, you are given the image measurements in inches, as well as the resolution of the image.

The program also offers additional information about the number of layers and alpha channels – about which you learn more later in this book.

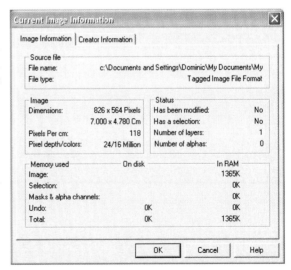

How do the images look?

Many programs display the required information immediately when the image is opened. The following dialog box of PhotoImpact 4 – which you can open by clicking *File/Open* – not only displays a preview of the selected image but also provides information about its size and resolution.

Information is only available when individual images are selected

In PhotoImpact 4, you can open a number of files simultaneously – a feature that is common in Windows programs. This way, however, no additional image information is displayed.

How to determine the appropriate resolution

Now you know about all of the important factors that are required to determine the perfect resolution for your image:

You learned that different resolutions have to be used for different output devices such as printers or monitors. Based on the monitor example, you now know how to easily calculate the resolution of an output device. The resolution of other output devices can be calculated in a similar manner.

33

2. The correct resolution and the best-suited color mode

The resolution of other output devices

You can calculate the resolution of other output devices in the same manner we calculated the screen resolution. Because these calculations are a lot more complicated, we forego them for now and spare you any further confusion. Simply use the values in the following table as a reference.

The table below summarizes the most important resolutions. You can find most of the current output devices with their corresponding resolution in it.

Resolution in dpi	Output device
37.5	300 dpi printer, 64 grayscales
53	300 dpi printer, 32 grayscales
75	Web sites, screen display
75	600 dpi printer
159	1,240 dpi Imagesetter (for book printing)
318	2,540-dpi-Imagesetter (for high-end book printing)

Working with the correct resolution

Let's assume you want to scan a photo that is 10 x 15 cm in size. Let's further assume that you want to scan the photo at the best possible quality. You might want to keep your options open and print the image as part of a book later on, just as we did in this book.

1 Start the image-editing program of your choice; you are using Corel PHOTO-PAINT™ for this example.

2 Open your TWAIN module. In this case, the commands used are *File/Acquire Image/Acquire*.

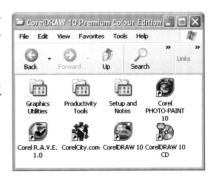

3 Make sure to set the correct resolution value. If you are using this program, you can use the *Resolution* list box for this purpose.

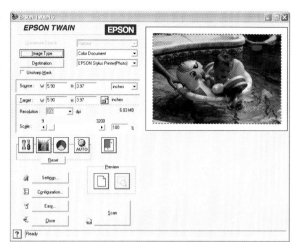

You can see from the table above that the resolution value required for this task – that is, book printing – is 300 dpi.

The resolution value is defined as dpi (**d**ots **p**er **i**nch) in the list box.

Rounded off values

In the table above, the resolution is given in exactly calculated values, for instance, 318 dpi. In practice, this value can be rounded off to 300 dpi.

4 Start the scanning process by clicking *Scan*.

5 Close your TWAIN module. The image is transferred to Corel PHOTO-PAINT afterwards, which you can see from the illustration.

2. The correct resolution and the best-suited color mode

The right display size

PHOTO-PAINT automatically adjusts the display size after the scanning process to make sure the entire image is visible in the work area. This option has to be selected in the presets, however.

6 If you go to *File/Document Info*, notice that the values are correct:

At a resolution of 300 dpi, the scanned image is of exactly the same size as the original photo.

Don't print the image because the image is too big.

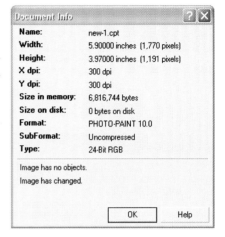

Document Info		? ☒
Name:	new-1.cpt	
Width:	5.90000 inches (1,770 pixels)	
Height:	3.97000 inches (1,191 pixels)	
X dpi:	300 dpi	
Y dpi:	300 dpi	
Size in memory:	6,816,744 bytes	
Size on disk:	0 bytes on disk	
Format:	PHOTO-PAINT 10.0	
SubFormat:	Uncompressed	
Type:	24-Bit RGB	

Image has no objects.
Image has changed.

OK   Help

7 Therefore, use the *Zoom* option of our TWAIN module to change the image size. Select *50%*. The resolution value does not change.

6.05 MB

3200

▶   50   %

8 The resolution is still maintained with this change; however, the image size has been reduced by half. The new measurements are displayed on the left side.

Resolution and target size

You now know that there is always a connection between resolution and size. At 300 dpi and 100%, the image would be printed in its original size and at optimum quality.

If you cut the resolution in half and maintained the scaling value, however, you would create an image of reduced quality: the pixels would be clearly visible. In addition, the image would still be 10 x 15 cm in size.

Which color mode would you like?

You must make one more decision: choose the color mode you would like to use. You can make your choice either when scanning the image or later on, when working in the image editing program of your choice.

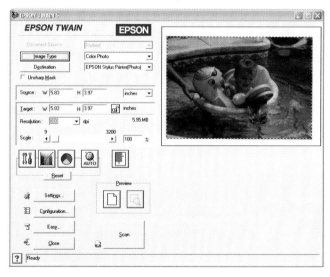

Because image-editing programs usually offer far more options than TWAIN modules, the latter method is recommended. Let's look at the options that image-editing programs provide. Corel PHOTO-PAINT™ 10 is used again for this purpose – other programs use a similar procedure, however.

Two colors are enough: Black & white images

The fist color mode to introduce is getting by with only two colors: black & white.

37

2. The correct resolution and the best-suited color mode

1 Go to *Image/Mode/Black and White (1-bit)* if you are using Corel PHOTO-PAINT™.

2 Use the values illustrated here for the conversion procedure.

3 The image only consists of black dots. The background creates the second color – white.

The impression of the image is dependent on the pattern of the black dots.

The color palette for the Web

You often come across a particular color mode when creating images for the Web: the palette mode. This mode offers you a maximum of 256 different shades of color.

1 Select the function *Image/Mode/Paletted (8-bit)*.

The dialog box illustrated allows you to select the number of colors – the maximum available value is 256.

The settings used are illustrated – the illustration uses 60 colors.

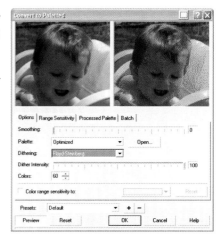

2 The *Processed Palette* tab allows you to view the colors used.

3 Even though a limited number of colors was chosen, the image is decent.

Selecting the right file format

As the GIF file format only supports 256 colors, it is suitable for creating images with 256 shades of colors. Because of the small number of colors used, it has a small file size and is therefore the standard file format for Web images.

Everything seems so gray – The grayscale mode

If you want to print images with a black-and-white printer, you can forego colors and save a lot of space on your hard disk.

Grayscale images also contain 256 different shades; however, only shades of gray are used in this mode.

No further options are available when converting the image. Go to *Image/Mode/Grayscale (8-bit)*, and the color image is automatically converted to a black-and-white image.

A perfect blaze of color: The TrueColor mode

If you are planning to present images on-screen, you should use the RGB color mode. The abbreviation stands for **r**ed, **g**reen and **b**lue – the colors composing each image.

This mode, which is also called TrueColor mode, allows you to use a maximum amount of 16.7 millions of different shades of color, 256 colors for each color channel. Do you want to view the image as it appears when separated into the different color channels?

Then open the *Channels* dialog window by selecting *Window/Dockers*, if it is not yet displayed in the right section of the work area. You can also use the keyboard shortcut Ctrl+F9.

Recognize the structure of the image from the symbols: each of the channels shows part of the subject of the image. The individual channels that are layered on top of each other, so to speak, create the colors you see on-screen. The image is therefore a combination of the three basic colors.

The standard color mode

You should generally choose this color mode when scanning images. You can always convert the image into another color mode – it doesn't work the other way around, however. If an image is scanned in black-and-white mode at the start, it cannot be converted back into a color image afterwards.

Perfect for printing: CMYK color mode

If you want to print your images, you must select another color mode, because prints are always made up of the colors cyan, magenta, yellow, and black.

Once you convert your image by using the function *Image/Mode/CMYK Color (32-bit)*, find the four corresponding color channels in the *Channels* window.

Some image editing programs do not support this color mode. Unfortunately, you cannot use these programs to create CMYK images; no alternative options exist in such a case.

Special color modes are geared towards the pros

Corel PHOTO-PAINT™ offers a number of special color modes such as duotone, multichannel or lab mode. You hardly ever need these color modes: they are usually intended for the professional user.

Some programs might offer additional color modes. PhotoImpact, for instance, offers a color table that is specialized for Web browsers. The basic color mode functions are usually the same in all programs, however.

Perfection: Great scans

Now that you've done some scans using the simple TWAIN module in the first chapter and simply accepting them the way they were acquired, this chapter is a little more challenging. You discover the possibilities available with the advanced options of the TWAIN module.

The appropriate software

For the image editing software, you can download one from the Internet in shareware format: Paint Shop Pro, which is currently available in version 7. This program is one of the most popular because it is one of the easiest to use. It also works quickly, something that is not true for many other image editing software.

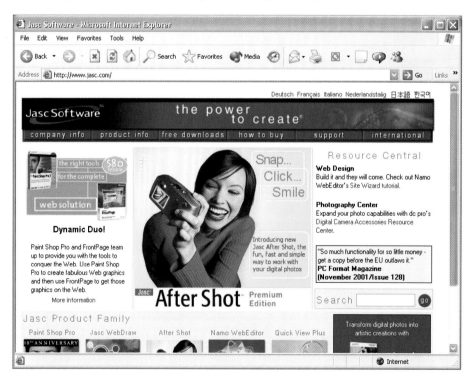

Paint Shop Pro is not absolutely free

Shareware programs are not free, as many users often believe. You can download a fully functional version of Paint Shop Pro from the Internet for trial purposes.

After trying it out for 30 days, you have to make a decision: If you like the program, you can purchase it at a very reasonable price. If you don't like it, you have to remove it from your hard drive.

After 60 days, you can no longer use the program without registering it; it simply won't function anymore.

Alternatives to the TWAIN module

If the TWAIN module that was included with your scanner doesn't offer you more advanced functions, work your way around this. Scan the image as best you can and edit it with the help of the functions available in an image-editing program. You'll learn more about it in the next chapter.

A rose by any other name ...

Be aware that the descriptions for your TWAIN module might sound a little different. Generally, however, the functions are as similar in name as they are in function to the ones used in this tutorial.

Let's have a look at what steps need to be taken to acquire an impressive scan:

1 Put the sample in the scanner so it is straight. Use the edges of the scanning surface as a guide.

2 Looking at the descriptions on the edge: you can find out how you should insert the sample so that it's not "standing on its head".

Always align the sample correctly

Correctly aligning the sample not only saves time, but also improves the image quality. Most image editing programs offer functions to correctly orient the image, but using them always diminishes the image quality, because all the image's pixels need to be recalculated. The result is usually somewhat less sharp.

3. Perfection: Great scans

3 Make sure the scanner is ready for use. Several models require a short warm-up time, whereas others are ready almost immediately.

4 Look for the icon belonging to Paint Shop Pro – it's either in the Windows Start menu or on the desktop.

5 Start Paint Shop Pro. You can see the still empty workspace in the following illustration.

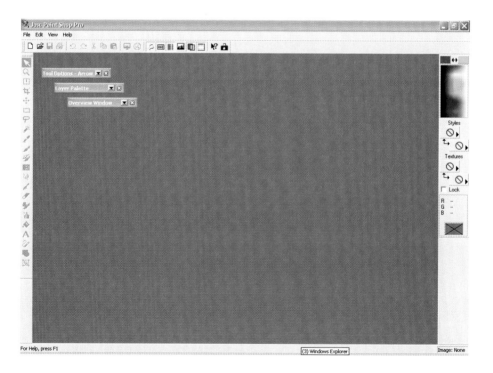

6 Go to *File/Import* and then to *TWAIN*.

7 In the menu, first choose *Select Source*.

8 In the dialog window, select the TWAIN module that offers the most functionality. In the example, it is Epson TWAIN 5.5.0 (32-32).

9 After confirming your choice, choose *Acquire* from the menu *File/Import/TWAIN*.

The already familiar TWAIN module starts.

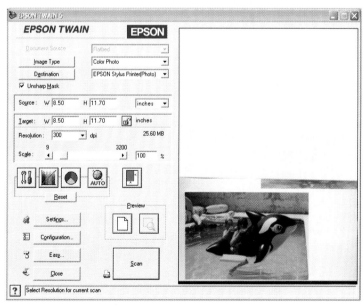

The right image area

Regardless of whether you are working with a simple or a complex TWAIN module, the first step is always the same. You must create a preview scan. With the example module, it's quite simple: When starting it, the preview is automatically displayed. It's a little different with some other programs:

1 To create a preview, click the *Preview* icon. Some other modules might also call this *Prescan*.

2 Afterwards, you'll see a tiny little picture with difficult-to-distinguish details in the preview area. After placing a marquee around the area to be scanned, another icon becomes active in the preview area. Use it to zoom into the selected area.

3 This useful function is often missing in simple TWAIN modules. After using this function, you can see the sample displayed larger.

4 The next thing you need is the icon shown here, which can be found above the preview icons.

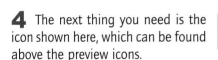

It is used to automatically find the edges of the image. This way you can save yourself the hassle of trying to correctly align the marquee.

5 Finally, you need the icon shown here, which can be found above the preview icons to the left. When you use it, the TWAIN module automatically determines the best values for optimizing the image. The preview image appears brighter and more brilliant.

Reasonable default settings

Our sample TWAIN module sets default values that automatically improve the quality of the image.

How to determine the best values

The preset values are good – but that doesn't mean better values can't be found. Therefore, consider the values that can be changed in the TWAIN module.

1 Because you are dealing with a picture that's a color image, leave the setting under *Image Type* as *Color Photo*.

Image Type	Color Photo ▼

CMYK scanner?

In the last chapter, you've already seen that for the printing of this book, the CMYK color mode was used. The CMYK setting appears in the list boxes of some TWAIN modules. You might therefore suppose that the scanner can scan in CMYK mode.

This is not the case: all scanners always scan in RGB mode. If you use the CMYK setting, the conversion most likely occurs within the TWAIN module. This way you can save doing the conversion in an image-editing program.

2 You've already seen all the important aspects about the resolution in the last chapter. In this example, set the default of 300 dpi under the description *EPSON Stylus Printer(Photo)*. Because our picture is quite big, scale the image down by 50%.

Destination	EPSON Stylus Printer(Photo) ▼
☑ Unsharp Mask	
Source : W 5.84	H 4.02	inches ▼
Target : W 2.92	H 2.01	inches
Resolution : 300 ▼ dpi	1.51MB
	9	3200
Scale : ◄	► 50 %

Improving the scan quality

The values found in the next area are also of interest; you can use them to influence the quality of the image. With the *Auto* setting you already used, the Epson TWAIN module determined the optimum values by itself.

Note

Quite often on target – but not always

In many cases, you probably get good results with the automatic optimization – but not with all samples. For example, imagine you want to scan an image where one color dominates. The program would automatically determine that this is a colorcast and automatically correct it. The result would then be incorrect.

Every image can be divided into various regions that can be optimized separately.

1 All areas in which many light image pixels are found are called "highlight areas". In this image, the highlight areas are where the light reflects.

2 The parts of the image where you see many dark pixels are called the shadow areas. In the example, a shadow area is the portion of the image with the face.

3 Use the first icon to open a dialog window where you can make adjustments for the highlights and the shadows. The adjustments can be made using the corresponding sliders or the text entry fields associated with them.

With the brightness value, set the overall brightness of the image; the gamma value determines the brightness of the midtones – the regions that are neither highlights nor shadows.

Using the preset values as a guide to making fine adjustments

When you start the TWAIN module, you find certain recommended values in the text input fields. Making fine adjustments to these values is easier than starting over completely with your own values.

4 Of particular interest are the options you obtain by clicking the second icon.

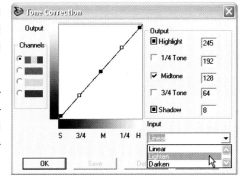

Several default values are available here, which you can optimize with the help of the list box. In the example, the *Lighten* option can improve the image.

You can also make changes to individual color channels to remove colorcasts. Adjust the color value curve in the preview by clicking it, or adjust the settings using the text input fields.

5 The last icon opens a dialog window in which you can remove colorcasts and change the values for the color saturation of the image. In the example, no changes are necessary.

6 Use *Reset* to set the values back to the original ones of the scanned in image.

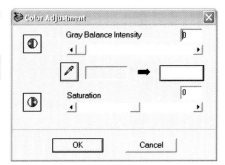

Reusing changed values

Perhaps you have many samples that should be optimized in the same way. It would be tedious of course to have to make the settings anew each time.

1 Click *Settings*.

2 The current settings are displayed in a specific region of the dialog window. Here, you can save the settings for future applications.

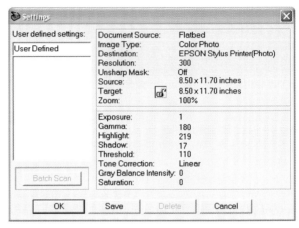

3 With the *Configuration* ...

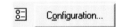

4 ... you can determine if the preview scan should be automatically acquired, for instance.

5 If you want to increase the sharpness of the image, you can disable the *Unsharp Mask* function.

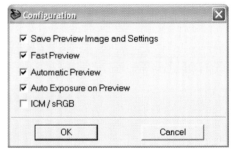

Because this can also be accomplished in the image-editing program, you should disable the function here.

Printed sample – but without the Moiré effect

There are still several special applications that the TWAIN module can be used for. These are described just briefly. If you want to scan in printed material such as magazines, for example, you encounter an undesirable pattern: the Moiré pattern.

This happens because printed material is composed of many small dots; you can see this if you use a magnifying glass and have a close look at some printed material.

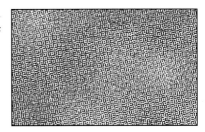

If these printed dots are scanned in and printed out again, the pattern in question occurs.

Note

Bad scanner – good results

It sounds a bit strange, but it's true: If you own a bad scanner, you have less trouble with Moiré patterns.

If the scans are little unclear, the Moiré pattern is less visible then in perfectly clear scans.

Many TWAIN modules include a function to reduce the Moiré effect; this is also the case with the program used here. This function is often called De-screening. You can get to this function by clicking *Image Type*. You can enable the function through the list box.

Several TWAIN modules also have a list of halftone frequencies to choose from. A lower value is good for scans from newspapers and a higher one for glossy material. You can't avoid making several attempts here.

You can use the following values as a rough guide – you're sure to reach your goal with them:

Raster value	For what?
175 lpi	art prints; used for high-quality prints
133 lpi	used for magazines, for example
85 lpi	used for newspapers

Last chance

If nothing else helps or your TWAIN module doesn't support these options, you can always improve the scanned images with the help of the tools found in an image-editing program.

First, use a feathering filter to make the image less sharp. Afterwards, you can sharpen the resulting image again using a sharpen filter. Of course this does not have a positive effect on the image quality, but that can't be avoided in this case.

Additional effects – additional conveniences

Depending on the TWAIN module you are using, further functions might be available. The module might offer color or special effects or something similar. Because most of these functions are also available in image-editing programs, they aren't necessarily required. The TWAIN module in our example doesn't have any of these functions at all.

That's it: Start the scan

Now that you have adjusted all the settings perfectly and saved them for next time, there's not much left to do until the scan is finished:

1 Click *Scan*.

2 It might be necessary for the scanner to go through a warm-up phase before it starts the actual scan.

Scanner is warming up. Please wait...

3 Wait a bit.

Depending on how large the image is – and the selected resolution – the scanning process can take a while.

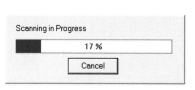

Scanning in Progress

17 %

Cancel

4 Once you have finished scanning the image, close the TWAIN module, because it is no longer needed.

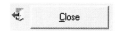

Close

The preview is retained

Most TWAIN modules retain the preview image when you start the module the next time. If you have placed a new sample in the scanner, you have to make a new preview scan. With our sample TWAIN module, set this option by clicking *Configuration*.

5 You then see the image in the editing area of Paint Shop Pro. The display size is automatically adjusted so that the entire image can be seen. The situation should now look like this:

Cropping images

You can still crop the image somewhat. Despite the automatic "image edge determining", a small border, which should be removed, can still be seen.

You can find the necessary tool in the toolbar on the left side – it looks almost the same in every program.

Drag the frame so that it encompasses the image area; you already know the process from the last chapter.

Even here you can still adjust the frame once you have dragged it to size. Double-clicking within the frame removes the contents outside the frame.

Saving images

To retain the completed work, you only need to save the image to the hard drive. Go to *File/Save As* or use the keyboard shortcut (F12).

The dialog window illustrated here then appears.

Select the desired file format from the *Save as type* list box; the BMP format is used here.

Universal file format

Because the BMP file format can be read by most image editing programs as well as other programs, it is a universal file format. Therefore, no problems occur if you want to incorporate the image into your text-editing program. Not much that can go wrong with choosing this file format.

Let's have a look at the results the optimized scanner settings gave us:

The image still contains some impurities: Spots occur in several places, as well as grainy parts and some scratches. These were damaged areas that were in the original image. You cannot make the necessary corrections using the TWAIN module, of course. You find out how to use the tools in an image-editing program to correct these problems in the chapter after next.

Optimizing bad images

In the previous chapters you learned about optimizing your scans by using your TWAIN module. This chapter teaches you how to optimize your images without using the TWAIN options.

Which image-editing program is the right one for you?

Before you can start to optimize your images, you need a program with which you can fulfill this task. Many different programs are on the market today.

The different programs offer different user concepts. Soap, for instance, is geared towards the novice user and is promoted as having an intuitive operation. Skilled users, however, miss a number of rudimentary functions.

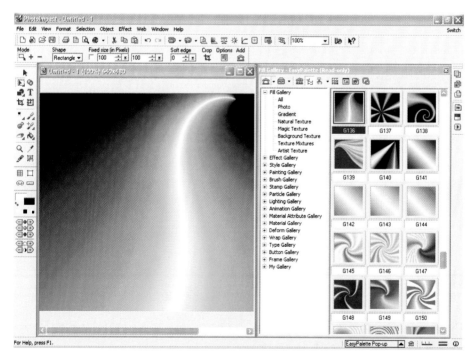

Ulead programs for the beginner

Ulead manufactures a number of popular and – in the meantime – widely used programs. PhotoImpact is the most popular of their programs. The program is easy to learn and offers extensive libraries that can be used by simple drag-and-drop actions. In addition, PhotoImpact offers many functions to create three-dimensional objects, which are particularly popular on Web sites, in a quick and easy way. The fast operation and the useful auxiliary programs that are added are quite impressive.

For the perfectionist: Photoshop

Photoshop – which is now available in version 6 – has become the standard image-editing program during the last couple of years. The current version contains an additional program called ImageReady, which offers many features for the creation of Web elements such as buttons and banners.

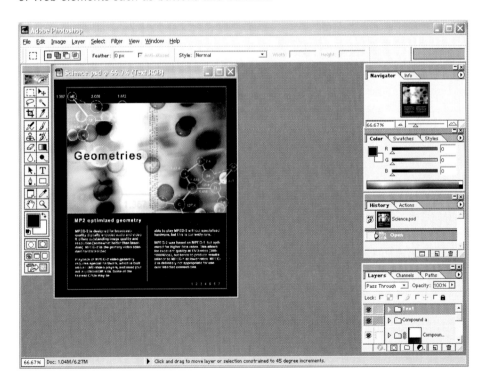

Beginners might have difficulties getting used to the rather unfamiliar work area, as the program was originally developed by Macintosh. Once you adapt to the somewhat different operation of the program, the program's strengths become evident: The developers spare you any claptraps – all functions are structured in a logical manner.

The high speed operation of the program, as well its precision and stability, convinces particularly professional image editors. Whereas other programs might be forced to give up when dealing with huge image files, you can certainly continue with Photoshop.

So ... which program is the right one?

There is no "right" image-editing program. It really depends on the task at hand. It is also a question of taste. If you want to use your scanned image to create an invitation in a quick and easy way, programs such as Ulead Photo Express, PhotoDeluxe, or Picture It! might be perfect for you.

More complex tasks probably require Micrografx Publisher or Paint Shop Pro. If you're doing professional work, you must use programs such as Corel PHOTO-PAINT™ or Photoshop. Ultimately, your choice depends on the price of the program – after all, programs like Soap can be bought for about $24.00, whereas you might pay $665 for Photoshop.

Optimizing bad scans

In the previous chapters, you have learned how to scan an image as best as possible. Your scanning results might not be successful, however – maybe because the original image was bad to start with or your TWAIN module does not support different settings.

You can see an unsuccessful scanning result in the next illustration.

Take a look at how you could improve such an image.

Again, Corel PHOTO-PAINT™ version 9 was used as the image-editing program here. The operation of the previous versions of the program is almost identical to this one.

Sample images from the Net

1 First, open the corresponding image by choosing the *Open* command from the *File* menu, or you can use the keyboard shortcut Ctrl+O.

2 Depending on the presets you previously chose in the *General* tab – which you can access by pressing Ctrl+J – the image is displayed at 100% or the program chooses the best fit. You can see that in the next illustration.

A consideration

As soon as you look at the image on the screen, you can tell that it is dull and too dark. But what if the image is actually okay and your screen settings are wrong? You would then unnecessarily modify the image – and even destroy a perfectly fine picture.

This is why many image-editing programs – such as Corel PHOTO-PAINT™ – offer an option to check the quality of images.

The truth about the image: The histogram

To find out about the actual quality of the image, follow the next steps:

1 Choose *Image/Histogram*.

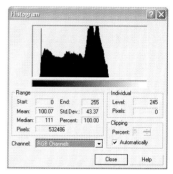

2 All pixels of the image are analyzed and plotted according to their frequency of occurrence in a diagram that is illustrated opposite. All dark pixels are displayed on the left side, and all light pixels are on the right side – the bar below the diagram indicates this allocation. The higher the "mountain" in the diagram, the more often does the corresponding luminosity value appear in the image.

3 In the case of perfect images, the mountain stretches over the width of the diagram evenly.

4 In the case of the sample image, the left and right section of the diagram displays no existing luminosity values – this indicates bad image quality. These gaps indicate that the image contains neither black pixels nor white ones – and that's exactly what a pro calls a "dull picture". The image does not have enough contrast.

Optimizing the fast way

You can be sure that the image is of bad quality, but what's next? Of course, Corel PHOTO-PAINT™ offers a way of correcting these flaws:

1 Choose the function *Image/Adjust/Contrast Enhancement*, which you can also call up by using the keyboard shortcut Ctrl+E.

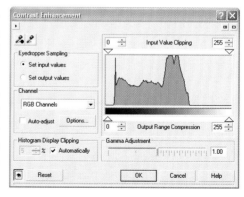

2 The corresponding dialog box displays another histogram, which almost looks like the previous one. The difference is that you cannot only look at the individual color values, you can also modify them now.

3 Enabling the *Auto-adjust* option that can be seen in the Channel section is the most convenient method.

4 Click *Preview* – at the bottom left of the dialog box – to view the effect on the original image.

5 You don't like the preview option because the processing of the original image takes too long? No problem. Click the left button in the header ...

6 ... to include the preview window in the dialog box. You now see the original image on the left and the modified image on the right.

7 This automatic adjustment produces a considerably better image. Is Corel PHOTO-PAINT™ doing magic tricks?

It almost seems like it: One click and you created a highly improved image from a bad one.

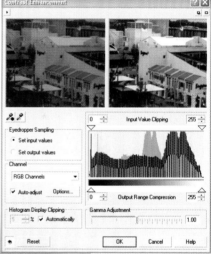

61

8 Choose *Image/Histogram* again and to see that pixels are allocated to all areas of the diagram now.

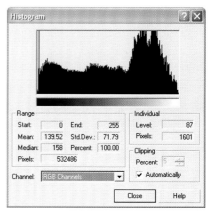

Correcting tonal values manually

Automatic features are great – as long as they do what you want them to do. As you already found out when you dealt with the TWAIN module, these automatic corrections also have their limitations. They do not work if your image contains large areas of consistent colors. All of a sudden your images might show an unwanted colorcast when you apply an automatic correction! Therefore, you must correct the image without the automatic function – and you quickly realize that there is no magic involved.

What are tonal values?

The different shades of color in an image can be indicated as tonal values.

Adjusting the midtones

The first step is to adjust the medium shades of color, the midtones of the image.

1 Let's start again with calling up the function *Image/ Adjust/Contrast Enhancement.*

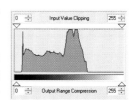

2 You can see two peaks in the diagram. The gray area indicates the data of the original image and the black line displays the modified values – at first, both lines are congruent.

3 To change the midtones, you must move the  *Gamma Adjustment* slider. If you increase the value above the default value of 1.0, the image becomes brighter. If you decrease the value below the default value, the image darkens.

4 Set the gamma value to 1.5. Notice that the new tonal value "mountain" was moved to the right. By selecting a new gamma value of 1.5, you have moved the "mountain" into the middle of the diagram.

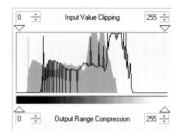

Increasing the contrast

After the image has been brightened, the contrast has to be increased. You already know that the empty tonal ranges at the right and left side of the diagram are the reasons for this flaw. So, simply cut off these areas:

1 Above the diagram, you can see two triangles as well as two data entry fields. Use these to "stretch" the mountain, so to speak.

Start with the value to the left. You can increase it until the empty areas are gone. In this example, the value 38 seems to be sufficient.

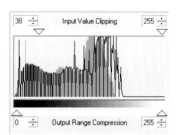

2 Repeat this step on the right side – the value has to be decreased to 196.

Notice that no empty areas remain at the left and right side of the diagram.

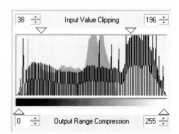

3 By carrying out these steps, you have clearly improved the image – it has a lot more contrast now. You have removed the grayness of the image. An expert would talk about increasing the luminosity of an image.

Color neutral – Removing colorcasts

Do you want to remove a slight colorcast from the image? Granted, it is not very strong – but the values displayed in the histogram prove it:

1 All previous steps were carried out with the *RGB Channels* setting in the *Channel* section.

2 As you learned in the previous chapters, images are made up of a number of color channels.

These can also be modified individually – choose a channel from the *Channel* list box. The red channel is illustrated on the left.

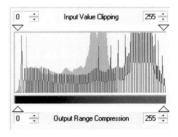

3 The green channel can be seen opposite.

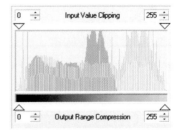

4 The colorcast is most noticeable in the blue channel.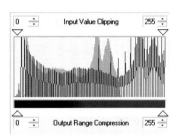

You can see in the diagram that parts are missing on the right side. These were cut off during the editing procedure of the overall channels.

5 You can remedy this flaw by using the text entry fields or the triangles below the diagram.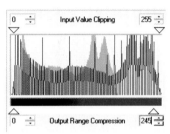

You can see the new values in the text entry field on the right. This way, the "lost" values were retrieved again.

6 Because of these changes, the image appears more neutral – the unwanted colorcast is now removed – as you can see from the image opposite.

Time for a change? – Changing values later on

Your changes were successful, but what do you do if you change your mind afterwards? That might be a challenge. Corel PHOTO-PAINT™ offers a special feature to change previously set values at any time: the lenses.

1 To create a new lens, choose *Object/Create/New Lens*.

2 You can choose the type of lens you want to use from the dialog box – this list also contains the previously used Contrast Enhancement.

Note

Changing lens values

If you want to change the values of a defined lens, select the command *Object/Edit Lens*. The same dialog box opens again, and you can now change the settings in this dialog box. Make sure that the corresponding object is selected in the *Objects* docker window when calling up this function; otherwise, the function is unavailable.

Adjusting image sharpness

The *New Lens* dialog box also contains the entry *Sharpen* – the following dialog box allows you to define the edge level. You can see the values on the left side.

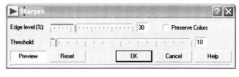

The *Objects* docker window contains three entries now: the background and the two lenses you selected before. The previous steps allow you to change your mind at any time – a useful function!

Now, our final result is finished.

You might still be asking, "So … what happened during the automatic adjustment?" Well, PHOTO-PAINT™ analyzes each color channel individually and cuts off empty sections. This way, any colorcasts are removed and the contrast is adjusted. A manual correction might prevent possible mistakes by the automatic function.

When all else fails: Retouching images

We've now spent enough time discussing how to optimize scanning in image samples. But if these steps are still not adequate in attaining the ideal image, you have to take a different approach. This is exactly where image retouching comes into play – the subject you'll be taking a closer look at in this chapter.

On the one hand, you can remove little impurities affecting the beauty of the image and, on the other, you can also manipulate the image considerably. This is how you can, for example, make it look as though you've been to Costa Rica, although you've actually never been there.

Scanning in slides

For the sample in this chapter uses a scanned in slide.

Additional attachments can be purchased for the scanning in of slides. You can see the transparency unit in our sample scanner illustrated here. When using such units, invert the slide and place it on the attachment – the same way you would with other scannable material.

A makeshift solution

If your scanner cannot be equipped with such a slide attachment, you can work around it: Light boxes can be obtained for the sorting of slides. Use such a light box by placing it on top of the slide during scanning. If the scanned image has stripes through it, rotate the light box by 90° so that the frequency of the light box and that of the scanner match up.

1 In the *Document Source* list box of the TWAIN module for Epson scanners, set the scanner for scanning in color negatives or slides.

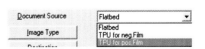

67

5. When all else fails: Retouching images

Removing the red tint

Although color negatives are masked with red, this red tint can be filtered out automatically by selecting the negative film option.

2 When scanning in slides, use as high a resolution as possible so that as many details as possible can be acquired. For example, use a resolution of 1200 dpi.

After you scan in the image, many things are worth improving, such as the overall image quality.

During scanning, some unwanted impurities and dust particles have become visible – which is somewhat annoying. In addition, we'd also like to make the sky look a little bit more interesting than just the one color tone.

Selecting an image editing program

It is actually irrelevant which image-editing program you use to perform the tasks at hand. The necessary tools are included in all the popular editing programs. Paint Shop Pro 7 is used in this illustration. Because this software can be downloaded from the Internet from *http://www.jasc.com*, you can reproduce each part of the example step for step. First open the image to be edited in Paint Shop Pro.

Installing Paint Shop Pro without an Internet connection

Do you not have a connection to the Internet? No problem. Have a look at some of the CDs included with computer magazines. The software is quite often included on these.

Setting the correct display size

Now you can get to work. First, you should ensure that the image is visible in its entirety. If the image fits into the workspace, Paint Shop Pro automatically displays it in its original size. If it doesn't fit, it is reduced until the image is completely visible.

The display size cannot be set arbitrarily

The display size in Paint Shop Pro cannot be set arbitrarily. The display size can only be altered in predefined levels that can be set in the View menu.

To change the display size to the original 1:1 size, proceed as follows:

1 The easiest way to set the display size is by using the  palette window *Tool Options – Zoom* illustrated here.

5. When all else fails: Retouching images

2 As soon as the mouse pointer is positioned over the title bar, the palette window opens. To change this default setting, click the arrow symbol on the right side of the title bar – the palette window always remains open then. Normally, it would close automatically once the mouse pointer is positioned outside of the palette window region.

3 Can you see the *Tool Options* palette window in the workspace? You must go to the View menu and select the *Toolbars* option. In the dialog window that opens, select which palettes/tool bars should be visible in the workspace.

4 To open the *Zoom* palette window, click the symbol at the far right in the palette window.

5 A menu appears from which you can select the *Zoom* option.

6 If the image doesn't fit onto the screen at a display of 1:1, you'll have to view it with the help of the scrollbars.

Global image correction

Sharing the image and adjusting its brightness and contrast is not discussed in individual steps here because it was already covered in the previous chapters. You can find the relevant commands for automatically correcting the image in the menu under *Colors/Histogram functions*.

Correcting areas with the Clone Brush

The first correction you undertake is removing any grains and specs of dust. Unfortunately, this cumbersome task is necessary with many scanned-in images. To perform this task, use the clone brush, which can be found in the toolbar to the left of the workspace.

1 Select the clone brush from the toolbar.

2 Additional settings are available for each of the tools, all of which can be made in the *Tool Options* palette window.

After you select the tool, the relevant options automatically appear there.

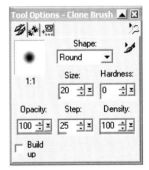

Changing the presets of tools

Before using a tool, first determine the correct settings.

1 With the preset values, you see only one symbol for the tool when drawing, such as the one of the clone brush on the left. With this setting, it is difficult to determine where you are drawing because the size of the brush is not recognizable.

2 It is therefore better if, in addition to the brush, its size can also been seen, as depicted on the left.

3 You can define these settings by going to the third tab in the *Tool Options* palette window. In that tab, enable the *Show brush outlines* option.

Employing the clone brush

What can you do with the clone brush? Work with it the same way you would with a normal brush – however, something is special about it:

1 If you move the mouse pointer over the image, notice the symbol illustrated here.

Move the mouse pointer to a place on the image where you don't see any grains in the sky – somewhere where it looks relatively clear. Then right-click.

2 With this step, you have to determine the source area.

3 If you click the imperfection once, notice that the sky is now being used as the drawing color. You can also see an X next to the mouse pointer. This brush in Paint Shop Pro isn't used to draw with a color but rather with another section of the image.

4 The X shows the section of the image that is being used to draw with – the source area that was previously defined.

Proceed to draw over each imperfection in the image bit by bit. When doing so, it doesn't matter whether you use dabs or strokes.

Undoing changes

You might occasionally make an error when drawing. What should you do if that happens?

1 Always keep an eye on the cross to see what it is you are drawing with. If you are not careful, you might draw with the wrong section of the image.

2 If you want to correct mishaps, you can go to the *Edit* menu and click *Undo*, or use the keyboard shortcut Ctrl+Z.

3 Perhaps you have already encountered the *Command History* option in the *Edit* menu? All the actions you have performed are listed there.

There you can see all of the individual strokes listed – this way you can completely delete all the brush strokes one by one.

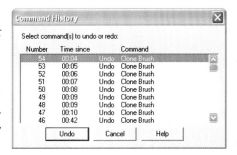

4 The source area is not rigid. You can place it elsewhere at any point in time. To do so, simply right-click another spot, press the button, and release it where you want to start retouching.

Note

Scrolling the image for assessment

View the image in an enlarged view so you can assess it. This way you are sure to notice other problems that you may wish to correct. Many of the imperfections that are not visible in the 1:1 display can then be eliminated.

You should undertake this process of assessment with every picture you scan in, even if it becomes cumbersome. Doing so makes the final image look much cleaner. The trouble is worth it!

5 Here you can see an illustration of the corrected image.

The first part of the task has been completed. We can now make our way to the second part.

Selecting image areas

In the second part of this tutorial, you must change the sky. Before you can do so, define the sky so that Paint Shop Pro knows in which areas to make changes.

1 For this task, you must make use of the *Magic Wand* tool.

2 Before you can use the Magic Wand, look at the *Tool Options* palette window.

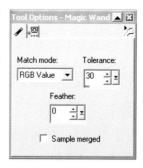

The *Tolerance* value is important here. It determines how similar the color values need to be before a selection is made – the higher the value, the less similar the colors need to be.

3 Now position the mouse pointer over the sky. Click the mouse once.

4 After doing so, notice a broken line representing the selecting region.

> **No line can be seen!**
>
> If you don't see a line, go to the Selections menu and see if the *Hide Marquee* option is enabled.

5 What happened when you clicked the image? Paint Shop Pro has taken into consideration the pixel you clicked and has selected all the pixels in the surrounding area that are of a similar color. Controlling the degree of similarity is accomplished with the definition of the tolerance value.

6 Perhaps you've already noticed this: Not all the areas in the sky were selected. Some sections in the left part of the sky were missed. Proceed to change the tolerance level to 20.

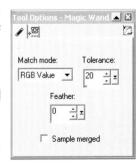

7 To include the missing section you must keep the (Shift) key depressed and click the image; otherwise, the existing selection is once again unselected. A plus symbol next to the normal Magic Wand cursor appears, indicating the *Grow* mode.

8 To include all the regions of the sky, some additional clicking with the mouse is necessary. Make sure that you successively click all the remaining regions of the sky while pressing (Shift).

9 To see the details of the back of the plane more closely, zoom into the image.

Inadvertent selections

If you have accidentally selected too large a section, simply undo the last step with the (Ctrl)+(Z) keyboard shortcut and set a lower tolerance value before clicking anything else.

More or less? – Changing selection areas

Selected areas are not permanent. You can continue adding to the selection or reduce it as desired. Use one of several available selection tools.

Identify additional tools in the toolbar for creating selected regions. You can, for example, make rectangular selections using the rectangular icon. The lasso (Freehand tool) allows you to select regions of any shape – and this is exactly the tool you are now going to use.

1 Before the selected area can be corrected, it first needs to be inverted. After all, you won't need the sky but the rest of the image.

To invert the selected area, use the *Selections/Invert* function; the keyboard shortcut (Shift)+(Ctrl)+(I) can also be used.

Several imperfections should now be corrected. Because of similar coloring, several jagged edges appear, for instance, by the wing.

2 The *Freehand* selection tool also has additional options in the *Tool Options* palette window. In the list box under *Selection type*, select the option *Point to Point*.

3 To remove areas from the current selection, you must press (Ctrl). A little minus symbol appears next to the mouse pointer showing that you are in subtraction mode.

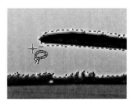

4 Click in the image. Use individual successive mouse clicks to define a closed-in area that encompasses the unnecessary selected regions. You can see this in the illustration.

5. When all else fails: Retouching images

Closing selected areas

If you have placed all the nodes, you must double-click to close the selected area. Paint Shop Pro then uses the node you last placed and the one you placed first.

5 Use this method to correct all the edge regions of the airplanes. Add or subtract the imperfect regions from the remaining selection. Also pay attention to the region underneath the airplanes.

The next illustration shows the mask once it has been corrected.

Saving selected areas

Selected areas only remain selected until you define a new selection. So that you don't have to do double the work, the completed selected area should always be saved.

1 To save it, go to *Selections/Save to Alpha Channel*. After you have clicked *OK* ...

2 ... you can assign a specific name to the alpha channel in the dialog window.

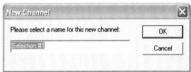

Watch the file format

When you're saving selected areas, you must ensure that the file format supports saving these. BMP files, for example, do not support alpha channels, whereas TIF does.

If you want to ensure that all Paint Shop Pro options you have used are supported, save it in Paint Shop Pro's own PSP format.

Working with layers

After you have created selections for the airplanes and the background, separate them from the rest of the image. You are going to, so to speak, delete the old sky. Therefore make use of layers. You can think of working with layers as having several screens placed one on top of one another.

On one screen, for example, you can see the sky, and on the one on top of it, the airplanes. This way you can simply replace the screen with the sky on it with another screen to behold a new sky.

5. When all else fails: Retouching images

This is exactly what you should do now.

1 Go to the *Selections/Promote to Layer* menu command or use the Shift+Ctrl+P keyboard shortcut. You then see a new entry in the *Layer Palette* window.

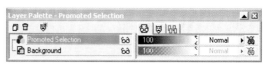

2 If you place the mouse pointer over the layer description, a preview image with the contents of the layer appears.

3 Click the eyeglass symbol located to the right of the *Background* entry.

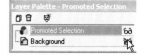

4 This removes the background. The marquee around the selected area has also been removed by using the keyboard shortcut Ctrl+D, because it is no longer required.

Instead of seeing the sky in the image, you now see only a checkered pattern. Paint Shop Pro uses this method to display areas of the image that are transparent.

In this step you reach the next intermediate goal: The old sky is no longer visible.

It does, however, still exist in the image. Clicking the symbol next to the *Background* entry once again reveals the layer containing it. In the last step, you insert a new sky.

Quickly importing new images by dragging and dropping them

Let's look at inserting a new sky into the image.

1 You chose the image shown here as the source of your new sky.

When selecting this image, ensure that the color is somewhat matched up with that of the previous image.

2 Open the image of the sky and position both images next to each other in the workspace.

3 Make sure that the active image is the one of the sky.

4 Switch to the *Layer Palette* window and click *Background*.

5 Press the mouse button and drag the layer to the other image.

6 Release the mouse button.

7 Notice in the *Layer Palette* window that Paint Shop Pro has automatically created a new layer.

8 Because the entry is listed above all the rest, the sky covers all the other layers.

You don't want this, of course – after all the sky belongs behind the airplanes.

Changing layer hierarchy by dragging and dropping

Even the changing of layer priorities can be easily accomplished with the mouse:

1 Click the newly inserted layer entry in the *Layer Palette* window and press mouse button.

2 Move the mouse pointer downwards, as illustrated here.

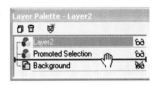

3 When you release the mouse button, the layer is inserted under the one promoted selection. You can then verify in the image that the priorities are correct – the sky is now behind the airplanes.

Moving layers to the correct position

After being inserted, the sky is placed arbitrarily in the image. The sky now has to be placed exactly in harmony with the rest of the image.

You need the *Mover* tool, which you can find in the toolbar.

1 If you click the image and keep the mouse button depressed, you can move the currently selected layer.

2 Once you have found the correct placement, release the mouse button.

3 That's it! The new sky looks more interesting than the old one, right?

You've completed all the tasks in this tutorial. And you did it using an image-editing program, costing slightly more than $100 for the registered version!

Note

Only with Paint Shop Pro?

The tutorial presented here can be repeated the same way, or at least in a similar fashion, with all popular image-editing programs.

Great uses for your scans

Is your scan done, optimized, and retouched?

This chapter shows you the different things you can do with your scans. Whether you want to create invitations, calendars, or other printed materials – learn how easily it's done. You can also put your scan on a Web page – as you find out in the first example.

Many programs offer you a large selection of interesting templates into which you can insert your scans. The number of such programs is growing: Picture It!, Adobe PhotoDeluxe, Kai's Soap and even such vector graphics programs as Windows Draw or CorelDRAW are all promising to make using your scans really easy.

Whether they keep their promise is what you'll discover in this chapter.

Optimizing scans for the Web

In the first tutorial, you needed to optimize a scanned picture for use on a Web site. To obtain an optimal result, keep a few things in mind.

Selecting the right resolution

Pictures on the Web are small, for the monitor screen has a very low resolution. Web images are a quarter of the size of printed images, as you already know from the third chapter.

1 With some TWAIN modules, the resolutions start at only 72 dpi – or just below, as in our example (50 dpi).

As long as you are using a small template, you should have no problem with this resolution; scanning a passport-sized picture for a Web site is easy enough.

Things get tougher if you want to scan a "normal" picture, however.

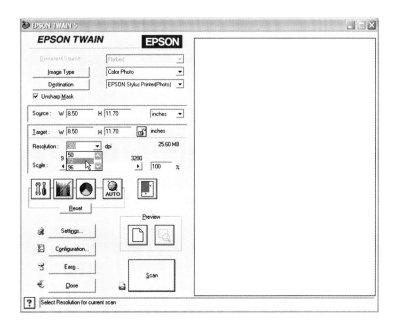

Note

For Web images, select a resolution of 72 dpi

The standard resolution for computer monitors is 72 dpi. Select this resolution, if you want to use the pictures for a Web site.

2 At a resolution of 72 dpi, a 10 x 15 cm picture would take up around 290 x 420 pixels on the screen. The image would be too large for a Web page, of course.

3 You could rescale the picture with the options available in the TWAIN module, but this is not recommended.

4 If you want to scan the perfect picture for your Web page, you should scan in the picture at least at double resolution.

5 Thus, if you want a picture with a width of 150 pixels, scan it with a width of at least 300 pixels.

85

Our sample picture is 282 x 417 pixels. The original picture was a standard 10 x 15 cm. You can scan a picture with these dimensions at 72 dpi without worries; in the end, you achieve exactly the desired dimensions.

Always scan your images larger than you need them

There are a number of advantages to scanning a picture that is double in size from the one you need. For instance, you can retouch pictures easier this way, because you can see the details better.

The quality of the image is also better, because the image is reduced afterwards. If you scan in the exact size you need, you loose details in the scanning process.

Reducing size after scanning

Because you have scanned the picture twice as large as you need it, you must now reduce its size. For this tutorial, you use the professional image-editing program Photoshop in its most current version (6.0).

The current version contains a few interesting Web functions to which you are now introduced. Editing pictures in other programs is similar, however; so you can go through the steps with any image-editing program.

1 In Photoshop, find the needed function in the *Image/Image Size* menu.

2 In the dialog window, enter the values shown on the left. This reduces the picture to 60% of its original size.

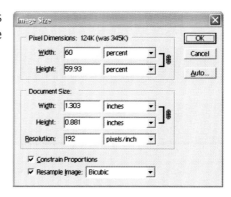

3 After resizing an image, you might want to correct the result ...

4 ... by going to *Filter/Sharpen/Unsharp Mask*.

5 Use the settings shown here.

6 Notice that when you apply the new dimensions, the resulting image takes a lot less space than the original. The new dimensions are perfect for Web publishing.

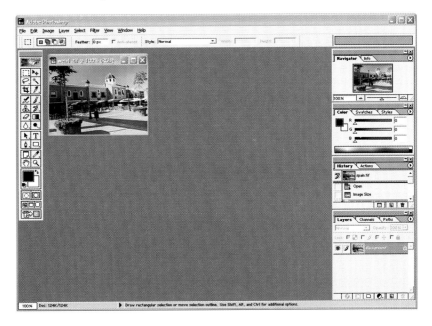

7 The quality of the reduced image is good. For the sake of comparison, see what the result would be if you scanned the picture directly in this size.

Even if the difference isn't huge, it is noticeable.

8 Before you edit the picture further, save it. To do so, go to *File/Save As* or press (Shift)+(Ctrl)+(S).

Save the image in the common TIF file format.

Optimizing images with ImageReady

Photoshop 6 comes with a second program called ImageReady. This program contains many functions for editing images for the Web. Unfortunately, the most useful functions aren't yet integrated into Photoshop – let's hope that this happens in the next version.

1 You don't need to go though the Windows Start menu to open ImageReady. Just click the icon illustrated on the left and located on the toolbar.

2 When you open the program, notice the many similarities between the editing windows. However unfortunately, some of the navigation elements are different from those in Photoshop.

3 Many of the palettes on the right side of the editing window are identical with those in Photoshop.

4 The image window shows a real difference. Above the image, you notice a number of tabs.

Switch to the *Optimized* view.

> **Note**
>
> **Always select JPG or GIF for the Web**
> You can use images on Web pages only if they are in JPG and GIF formats. Because both file formats cause a loss in quality, you should back up your picture in a loss-free format like BMP as well.

Changing the optimization settings

You have different options for both Web file formats. For GIF files, for instance, you can determine how many colors your image should contain.

1 For JPG files, you have only a few options. They are located on the *Optimize* palette.

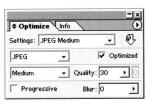

2 Select the desired file format from the list box. PNG is a relatively new format that is not commonly used yet and therefore not recommended.

3 In the next list box, select the degree of quality. There are four predetermined quality levels.

4 If you want to enter a more exact compression factor, use the *Quality* text entry field. Here, you can type in the compression rate.

As an alternative, you can also use the slider that appears when you click the arrow next to the text entry field.

5 When you set new values, the image in the *Optimized* view is refreshed. This way, you can always see the effects of changing the different values.

Saving and checking a JPG image

After you have found the right optimization values, save the optimized version of the image. To do so, proceed as follow:

1 In the *File* menu, identify the different *Save* options.

To save the picture with the properties you assigned to it in the *Optimize* palette, go to *File/Save Optimized As*.

2 In the dialog window that opens, select whether you also want to create an HTML file with your image.

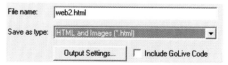

3 If you want to see a preview of the HTML file, go to *File/Preview In*.

In the menu, find a list of the Web browsers installed on your computer.

4 In addition to the picture, you also see the HTML source text, which was automatically created.

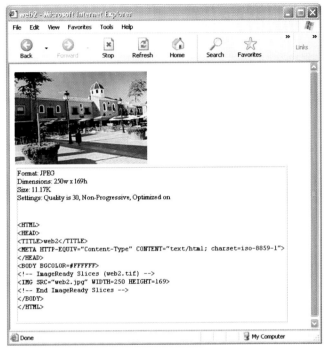

You don't need to save the preview

You don't necessarily need to save the file to use the preview option. ImageReady creates temporary files for the preview, which are removed again after you close the browser.

Beautiful frames with Ulead PhotoImpact

Next, you can add a beautiful frame to a scanned image. Then, you can use the result as a card or even a poster.

For this, use the program PhotoImpact, which is currently available in version 7. To download a trial version from the Web, go to *http://www.ulead.com*.

6. Great uses for your scans

1 Open PhotoImpact and go to *File/Open* or press Ctrl+O.

2 Notice the preview image that shows you what hides behind each file name.

We have selected a previously optimized scan.

3 Go to *Window/Tile with EasyPalette* and select the layout shown on the left.

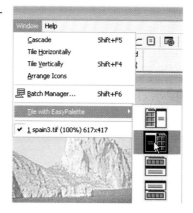

Practical palette for easy editing

All templates offered by PhotoImpact are located in the EasyPalette window. Here, you can find backgrounds as well as effect filters and lighting effects.

It makes sense to leave the EasyPalette window open at all times, because you definitely use it very often.

Note

4 Click the first button in the EasyPalette window to go to the *Frame Gallery*.

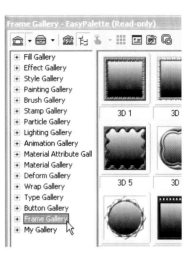

The EasyPalette window is now located on the right of the open image.

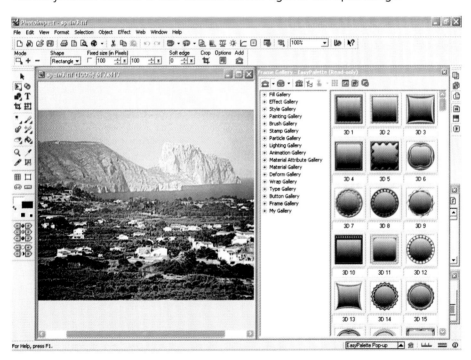

Framing a picture

Now we want to apply a frame from the easy EasyPalette window to our picture. Proceed as follows:

1 The individual frames are divided into different categories, which you can reach by clicking the tabs.

2 In the *Classic* category, you can find a couple of 3D frames.

3 Click the thumbnail of the frame on the left and press the mouse button.

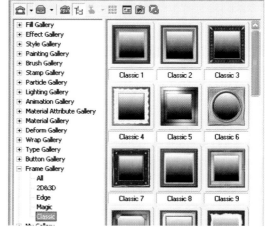

4 Drag the pointer into the picture.

5 Release the mouse button, and the frame is applied to the picture. Notice the interesting result.

Dragging and dropping frames
The fast assignment of frames by dragging and dropping is practical. You can even apply effect filters this way, unlike with many other programs.

Advanced options

Assigning effects as shown is easy. You do have the option, however, of customizing the default settings.

1 Go to *Format/Frame & Shadow*.

In the dialog window, you can change all the frame properties (such as width and shape).

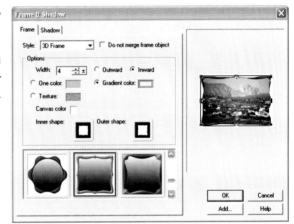

2 To change the gradient, click the small thumbnail next to the *Gradient color* option. The dialog window illustrated here opens.

Here, you can change the gradient type and orientation.

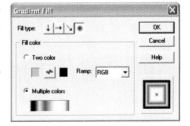

3 Click the thumbnail underneath *Multiple colors* to customize the gradient colors.

A separate dialog window opens, in which you can either select new color combinations from the list of predetermined colors or change the existing selection.

4 When you have made all the desired changes, click *Add* to save the new values.

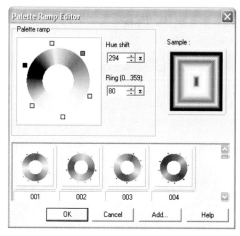

5 You can see the result.

Photo business cards in no time

In the following example, you insert a picture in a business card. For this example, use DATA BECKER's 30,000 Business Cards. As implied, this program offers a large selection of templates for business cards – both for personal and business purposes – into which you can insert your pictures.

1 When you open the program for the first time, you can choose whether you want the selection to appear as a directory tree or grouped by different categories. The tree view is shown here.

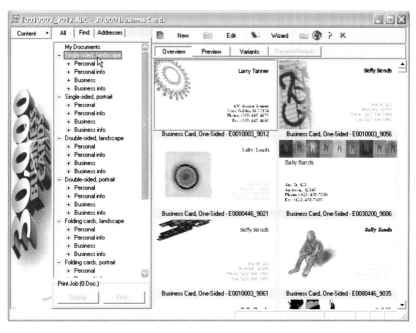

From the directory, select the *Single-sided, landscape* layout.

2 For each layout, you have a choice of *Personal*, *Personal info*, *Business* and *Business info* templates. Select *Personal*, then click the little plus sign in front of the entry to view the three styles available for this type. Select the *Background* style.

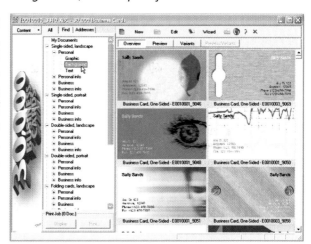

6. Great uses for your scans

3 Notice that the preview images on the right side of the program window have changed. These are now the personal business cards with a background. Scroll down until you encounter the template illustrated here (3310). Click it to select it.

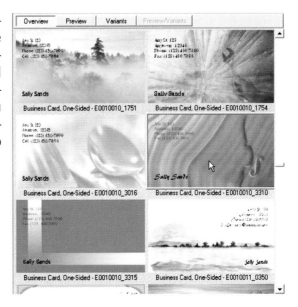

4 Each template comes in different versions, which you can view by clicking *Variants* above the images. Once you have found a variant that appeals to you, double-click it.

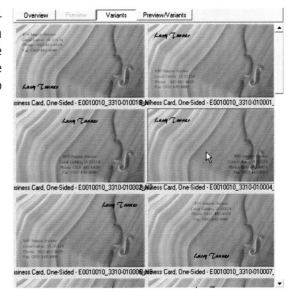

The template now opens in a new window, where you can make the necessary changes.

In the toolbar on the left, click the *Edit Text* icon to make changes to the text.

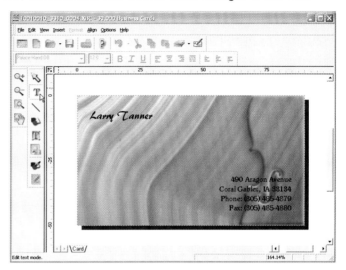

5 Click the text you want to change. The selected text block appears in a selection box. Within it, you can highlight the text you want to change and then type over it.

In the upper portion of the dialog window, find the options for formatting the text. To change the color of the text, go to *Format/Color* to reach a palette from which you can select the desired color.

In the lower portion of the window, a preview displays the results.

6 You can edit the other text blocks in the same way. To select a new text block, click it. You can recognize the new selection by the selection box around it.

7 Work through all text blocks step by step until you have changed all texts. On the left, you can see how the end result would look.

Inserting your picture

Now we want to insert a picture into the business card to make it even more personal. Because there is no template for the picture, you can place it anywhere you want.

1 To insert a picture, go to *Insert/Import Image.*

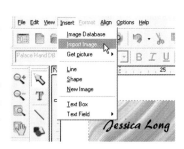

2 In the window that opens, browse for the directory in which your picture is located; then select the picture by clicking it. Click *Open* to insert your picture.

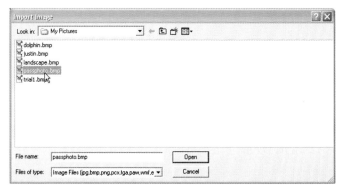

3 After you position your photo by dragging it to the desired spot, click the *Edit Image* icon to edit the picture.

4 A separate window opens, in which you can edit the image as you would in an image-editing program.

When you are done, save and print your work.

Duplicating passport pictures

You can print out your passport pictures with any program you want. For the example, a practical utility from DATA BECKER is used called Perfect Photo Printer. You can find more information on this product on DATA BECKER's homepage at *http://www.databecker.com.*

1 Start the program. A Wizard appears that takes you through the necessary steps.

Select the option *Start a new project.*

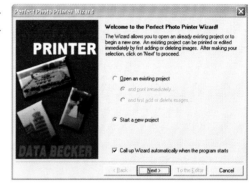

2 In the next step, you need to select the paper you want to use.

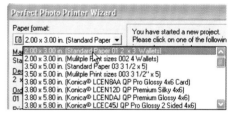

3 Click the *File(s)* icon to load the picture you want to print.

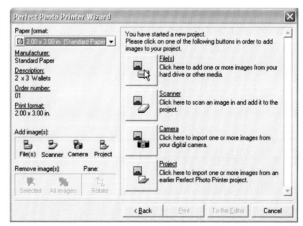

4 After the selection, a preview image of the selected picture appears in the browser.

Switch to the *Browser* tab to view all pictures in the selected directory as thumbnails.

5 After you make your selection, return to the Wizard.

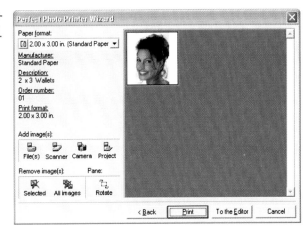

Optimizing images

Perfect Photo Printer has the advantage that you can do more than just print out the selected pictures. You can also optimize the image without needing a separate image-editing program.

Among other things, you can change the brightness, contrast and Gamma value, as well as the sharpness of the image. You can also automatically correct small mistakes.

For your convenience: Perfect Photo Printer from DATA BECKER

If you print out pictures only occasionally and without editing them much beforehand, such a utility is a worthwhile investment. This way, you can save yourself the burden of learning the many functions of image editing programs.

6. Great uses for your scans

1 To edit the image, click *To the Editor* to open the editing window illustrated below.

2 Underneath the preview image on the left, locate a few sliders for correcting the image. The list boxes underneath them contain a few preset automatic corrections.

3 The first slider regulates the contrast, the third the brightness of the image. Use the third slider to heighten or lower the sharpness. The last slider controls the Gamma value.

You can see all changes you are making in the image.

4 Click the diskette icon to save your settings. This way, you don't need to change all values from scratch for additional pictures.

5 If the subject of your picture has red eyes, you can neutralize them by going to *Edit/'Red Eye' filter*.

You can make the correction in the dialog window below.

6 Once you have optimized your picture, go to *File/Print*.

Set the number of printouts in the illustrated dialog window. To do so, click the number display underneath the picture on the left. Select the number of printouts from the list box.

If you load several pictures, they are all displayed in this dialog window. We have selected only one picture, so the dialog window appears nearly empty.

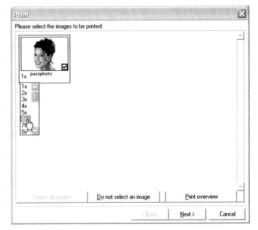

7 Click *Next* to reach the last dialog window, where you can set up the printer.

Enable the option *Print cut lines*, so that it is easier to cut out the picture after printing it.

Adjusting the printer

Before starting to print, you should adjust the printer so that your printout is neatly positioned on the paper. To do so, use the corresponding buttons. A Wizard takes you through the necessary steps.

Printing a CD cover

If you want to print CD covers and labels, you could use another DATA BECKER program: "5,000 CD & DVD Designs". It's introduced here by means of a little example.

In addition to the program CD, the bundle includes some trial paper for printing out CD covers. For this program, too, you need to adjust the printer before you begin.

1 After you install and start the program, a Wizard opens.

In the first step, determine the type of CD. For instance, if you need an audio CD cover, you can automatically read in the titles and place them on the CD insert.

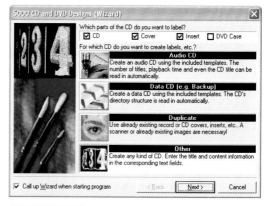

2 In the second step, you need to enter the CD title and some other textual information.

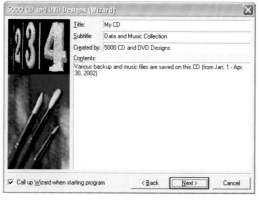

3 Next, you can select the desired design. The program CD includes many different attractive templates. Browse through them to get an overview.

On the left, notice the selected theme for the CD label.

4 In the other tabs you can see that the theme and font were automatically applied to the CD cover ...

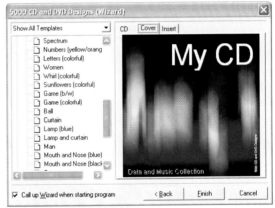

5 ... as well as the insert.

Click *Finish*. A message reminds you that you could start printing at this point. Otherwise, you can edit your design further.

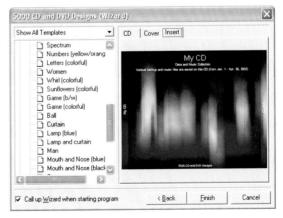

6. Great uses for your scans

6 In editing mode, you can edit the font, for instance. Click the object you want to change; locate the necessary functions in the toolbar.

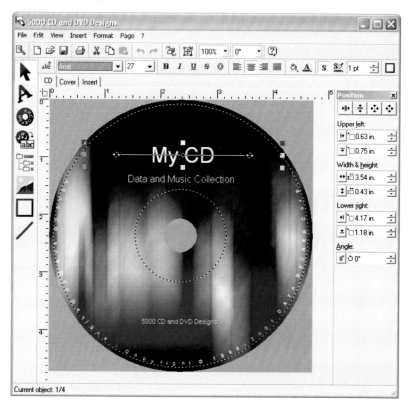

7 You can insert your own photographs with the function *Insert/Image File*. Use the demarcations to adapt the size of the imported picture. Press (Shift) when you scale the picture to keep the same aspect ratio.

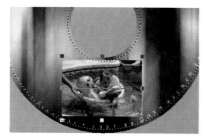

You can enter precise numerical values for positioning, scaling, and rotating the picture in the text entry fields on the right.

Printing the result

Finally, print out the three parts of the CD. You can print them all at once:

1 Go to *File/Print* or press Ctrl+P.

The first dialog window displays a preview of the three parts of the CD one more time. Check the parts you want to print.

2 In the second step, a prompt asks what kinds of paper you want to use for the cover, label, and insert.

3 In the last dialog window, adjust the printer. The preview images guide you to the correct positioning of the paper.

Finally, press *Print* to start the printing process.

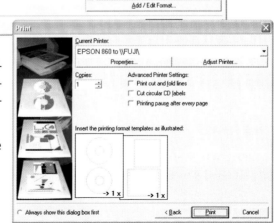

Using the scanner as a copying machine

You need a photocopy of a document and have no color copier?

No problem. Use your scanner in combination with your laser printer. You can copy documents using your scanner by going through the steps for creating and printing a 300 dpi scan.

However, you can also use some shortcuts. Some manufacturers offer software solutions for this task. Some scanners even come with a corresponding utility. The Epson scanner used here is one of them.

Calling up the program at the touch of a button

The Epson scanner simplifies the work further through the buttons on the front of the scanner. To call up the Help program, press the corresponding button.

1 To reach the copying function, go to the Epson Smart Panel. Here you can find different special Help programs.

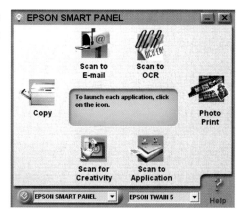

2 To "photocopy" a document, place it on the scanning surface and call up the *Copy* function.

3 This starts a program with an interface similar to the design of a photocopier.

Use the buttons underneath the display to set the size and number of the copies.

Use the display to adjust the printer settings.

4 Open the "lid" on the left, next to the *Start* button, to see the additional functions. Here, you can adjust the copy quality, for instance.

5 Click the green *Copy* button to start the copying process. The program automatically scans the entire scan surface ...

... and prints out the result on the selected printer. You don't have to do anything else.

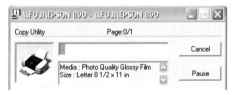

No saving necessary

This procedure has the additional advantage of saving disk space, for you don't need to save the result. The file that was temporarily created is automatically deleted once the printout is completed.

Faxing and mailing using the scanner

There are also special utilities or programs for faxing and mailing using the scanner.
Once again, the task at hand requires preparing the scanned images automatically.

1 Select the *Scan to E-mail* option from the Epson Smart Panel to start
the e-mailing utility.

**Scan to
E-mail**

2 Start the preview and select the desired area.

On the right, you can make the necessary adjustments. The options are self-explana-
tory.

3 The program automatically adjusts the settings corresponding to the option you choose
under *Type of Document*. For instance, the program helps you avoid moirés for scanned maga-
zine pages.

4 Click *Scan* to start the scanning process
with the selected settings.

Note

Correction possibilities

If you want to make your own corrections, start your old friend, the TWAIN module, by clicking the TWAIN button. Make the necessary adjustments there.

5 An overview page shows you your scan.

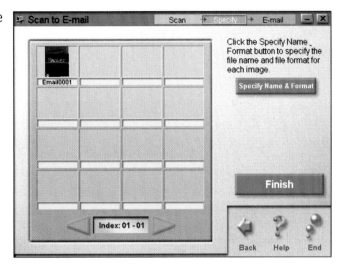

6 Click *Specify Name & Format* to select the desired file type in the corresponding dialog window. You can also customize the file name.

7 Click *Options* ...

8 ... to set the degree of compression. The higher you set the quality, the larger the created file is and the longer it takes to send the e-mail.

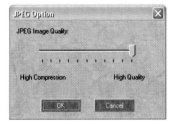

6. Great uses for your scans

9 In the last step, determine the e-mail program with which you want to send the image.

After you confirm your selection, the e-mail program ...

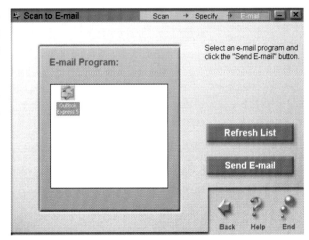

... is automatically opened. Enter the recipient. The attachment directory shows that the scan is e-mailed in the selected file format.

3D scans

In the last example, try to scan a three-dimensional object, because you can place more than just two-dimensional objects on the scanner.

No "depth"

Because the scanner doesn't work with an optical lens, as cameras do, the natural depth of photographs is missing. Objects that are further away appear blurry. Three-dimensional objects therefore look somewhat "flat" when scanned.

114

1 Gather together different coins and spread them on the surface of the scanner. You can even stack them if you want.

2 Start the image-editing program and make the usual adjustments in the settings of the TWAIN module. Next, edit the result in Photoshop.

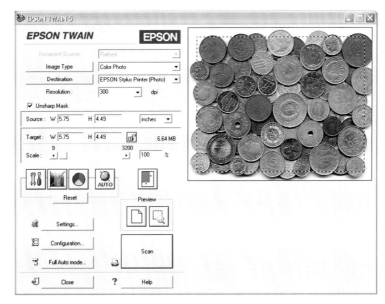

3 After the scan, optimize the result. The first temporary result is illustrated on the left.

6. Great uses for your scans

4 To balance the contrast and brightness, go to *Image/Adjust/Levels* or press Ctrl+L.

Use the *Auto* function with which Photoshop determines the optimal settings automatically.

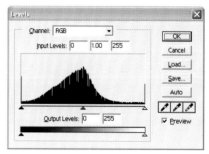

5 To make your few colors look richer, go to *Image/Adjust/Hue/Saturation* or press Ctrl+U.

In the *Saturation* field, raise the value up to 30.

6 If necessary, you can balance the sharpness of the image by going to *Filter/Sharpen/Unsharp Mask*.

7 These changes finally result in this image.

Similar working steps

The functions presented here might be called something else in other image-editing programs; however, the basic editing steps are identical.

116

Everything in tune: Calibrating your devices

It's a well-known problem: you have a scanner, a monitor, and a color printer, and nothing should stand in the way of perfect images. Yet in reality it looks different: the printout barely resembles the original image. How can you avoid this?

The professionals tell you that it's all about (fine) tuning: all devices, from the scanner to the monitor to the proofing device to the color printer are perfectly in tune with each other. This process is called calibrating.

Even though professional calibrating systems are out of reach for the home user or the aspiring professional, you have other ways to ensure a good resemblance between the original and the printout. The task is clear: a color original (for example, a four-color photograph) should result in a color printout where the printout is as close to the original as possible.

The right template for calibrating

The one indispensable prerequisite for a calibration that really works is using a template with the right motif. But how do you come by the right motif?

Many image-editing programs (or at least the expensive ones) come with color charts for calibrating the scanner and TIF files for calibrating the monitor. Corel, for instance, has been including such color plates for many versions now. If you don't have such a color plate, you can get one from a good photography store.

If you don't have a color plate, you can make one yourself. To do so, you need a vector graphics or image-editing program, however.

In the vector graphics program (for example, CorelDRAW), create a graphic containing squares as illustrated. Fill in each square with a different color. Make sure to include a full range of tints for each color.

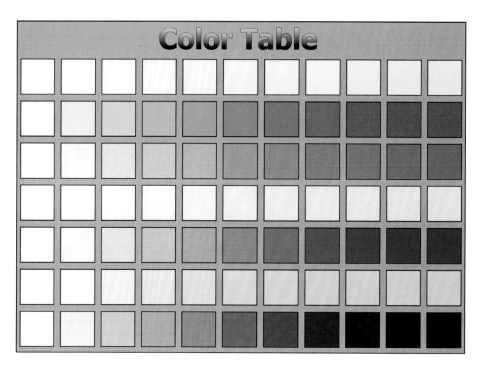

Calibrating the scanner

Now you can start the actual calibration. To do so, first scan in the color chart with the scanner.

1 When scanning, first use the default settings. This often puts you closest to the best result, for the manufacturers have already adjusted the default settings so you don't need to make many changes.

2 Make sure to choose a scanning resolution that is high enough for you to evaluate the printout without much difficulty. You already know that the standard resolution is of 300 dpi.

3 Once the TWAIN module sends the image to the image-editing program, check the colors of the picture. All image-editing programs have a tool with which you can sample the colors in an image.

In Paint Shop Pro, the color sampling tool looks like this. In addition, image-editing programs usually contain an option for displaying color values. In Paint Shop Pro, this display is a tag that appears next to the mouse pointer.

4 In the illustration, the pointer is hovering over a red field. The red value (*R*) is therefore 255, which is the maximum value. The green and blue values, on the other hand, are 0, which means that the color is pure red—the ideal case.

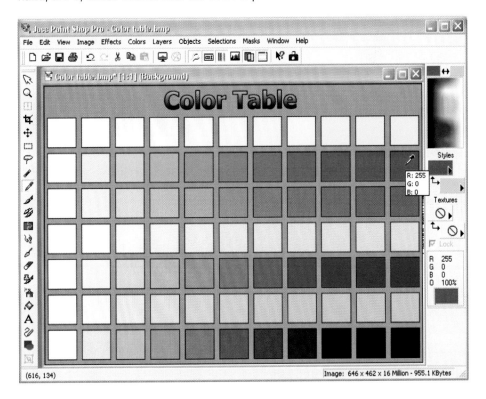

5 However, more often than not, the red field contains different values, like 240/10/9.

6 In this case, your scanner has produced a colorcast, which is what we want to correct here.

Pure colors

Color values are measured from 0 to 255. 255/255/255 is pure white and 0/0/0 is saturated black. 0/255/0 means that there are 0 parts red, 255 parts green and 0 parts blue contained in the color.

Correcting color casts

If you find out that a colorcast was produced during scanning, proceed in the following manner:

1 You might think that the color fields should be used to correct this fault. However, it is much easier to evaluate a colorcast with the help of a white or gray field.

2 Place the eyedropper pointer over one of the gray fields.

3 If the RGB values aren't identical, you have a colorcast. Fields without colorcasts always have identical values for red, green, and blue.

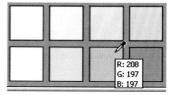

4 The values in the example disclose a red cast (the red value is higher than the other two values by 11). To correct the color cast, switch to your TWAIN module and search for a tint changing option.

 No values, no calibration

If your TWAIN module doesn't offer any options for changing the tint, you have no choice but to make changes later with an image-editing program.

5 The tint changing option might differ widely from TWAIN module to TWAIN module. Some programs offer this kind of histograms, for instance.

In this case, you can change the tint with the help of the illustrated icon.

6 Before you get to the tint correction, you must activate the corresponding option in the *Image Type* dialog box.

7 In the *Color Adjustment* dialog window, you can import a color tint with the eyedropper and adjust the RGB value with the help of the slider.

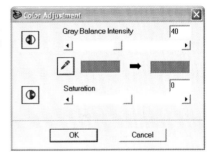

8 After correcting the value, you must scan and check the color chart once again.

Repeat these steps until absolutely no colorcast remains in the neutral gray.

9 If there is no colorcast in the gray, there shouldn't be one in the color fields, either. If this is not the case, adjust the tints in the other fields in the same way.

Writing down the values

If you have found the right values, write them down, for you cannot save them in the TWAIN module.

Calibrating the printer

If you have an optimally scanned color table, you can dedicate yourself to the next task: calibrating the printer. To do so, use the scanned image of the color table. It is even better, however, to use a constructed image like the color table, to be sure that you have the right color values.

The procedure is similar to the one just described – except this time you're starting at the other end.

1 Almost all image-editing programs have a *Print* option in the *File* menu.

2 In PhotoImpact 7, the following dialog window appears when you go to *File/Print*. In some programs, this dialog window contains many options, in some only a few.

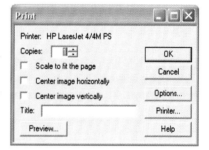

3 Select the printer you want to use (in our case, it is an Epson printer).

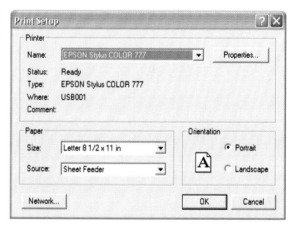

4 Depending which printer you are using, you have different options for balancing the printout.

Here, too, the following applies: if the printer driver doesn't have any options for the settings you need, you cannot calibrate the printer.

If all else fails

If your printer driver doesn't come with the necessary options and there are no options for adjusting the settings in the image-editing program, you need to proceed in an unorthodox manner. For instance, if the printout is too dark, you must simply brighten the picture. This is a less satisfying method, however, because it means changing image data.

5 PhotoImpact 7 offers you an interesting calibration function among the print options – an amazing possibility for such a price-worthy program.

6 Here, you can adjust the individual color channels by changing the curve.

7 For the first test printing, use the default values again.

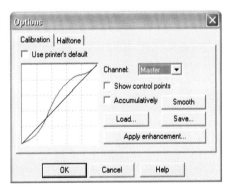

123

Analyzing the printout

You must now check the first printout. The goal, once again, is to obtain gray fields without a colorcast once again.

1 Look at one of the white fields.

2 Check if you can see any colored dots in it. If you can't make that out with the naked eye, use a magnifying glass.

3 If you notice that there are red dots in one of the white fields, for instance, the printout has a red cast.

4 In your printer driver, search for the correction options. In the example, the correction is undertaken in the illustrated dialog window.

If you have found only a few small dots, the correction value you must enter is small. The larger the dots, the higher the correction value you must enter.

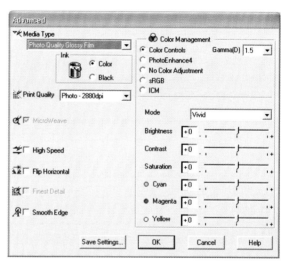

Measuring instruments make a difference

Unless you have an indecently expensive measuring instrument called a densitometer, you have no choice but to calibrate by trial-and-error.

5 Only when the white fields are really white can you dedicate yourself to the color tints. Make sure that there are no holes in the pure hues on the right. The right color fields should be continuous color surfaces.

6 Cyan, magenta, and yellow are the only solid colors; the rest of the hues are combinations of these colors.

Using the driver options

You should really try to make corrections using the options provided by your printer driver. Why? For a simple reason: when you switch programs and print from another program, you need to change the settings again. However, if you use the driver settings, everything stays the same, for you are using the same driver.

7 If the darkest and lightest areas are all right, check if the gradations happen in more or less equal steps. If this is not the case, you must adjust the contrast settings.

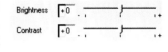

8 Because you are using only your naked eyes, the evaluation of the contrast is probably going to be difficult.

You should make sure, however, that each color field is different from the next. If the first three or last three fields are white, for instance, too much contrast results.

The right order is important during calibration

The right order of the procedure is important during calibration. Only when the color chart is printed perfectly can you use other motifs. It is harder to analyze a normal picture than it is to analyze a color chart.

In addition, make sure that you only optimize one feature at a time. Otherwise, you won't know which setting is responsible for the result, so you're better off making more printouts!

Calibrating the monitor

Now, you only need to calibrate the monitor, the link between the input and output devices. After all, this is where you decide whether you like the result of the scan or not.

1 Here, too, it is best if you adjust the original driver of the graphics card.

The only problem: only a few graphics cards come with a calibration tool.

7. Everything in tune: Calibrating your devices

2 In addition, you have the difficult task once again of evaluating the image without the assistance of measuring tools (which are out of the range of the average user).

3 To find out if your graphics card comes with a calibration tool, right-click an empty space on the Windows desktop and select the *Properties* option from the menu.

4 The *Settings* tab contains information on the monitor and the graphics card. You might even have a separate tab for your graphics card – in our example, this is not the case.

5 In an ideal case, you can find options for setting the brightness, contrast, and Gamma value on this tab.

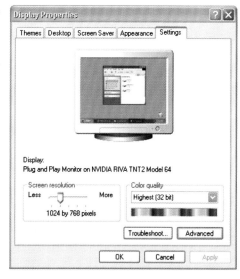

Applicable for all programs

If you are using this possibility, you have the advantage that the settings you adjust are applicable for all programs you are using, whether they are text or image-editing programs.

Display calibration with PhotoImpact

If your hardware doesn't offer you any calibration options, adjust the settings in the image-editing program you are using.

126

Here are the options in PhotoImpact (other programs function in a similar way).

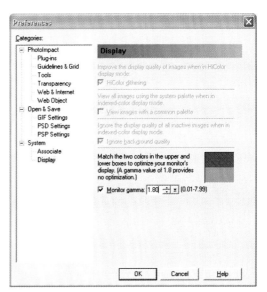

1 Go to *File/Preferences* or press [F6].

2 Choose *System/Display*.

Here, you see two gray fields. If they are the same shade of gray, the Gamma value is correct.

Otherwise, you must change the value by typing a new one into the text entry field.

3 To brighten the picture, enter a value higher than 1.8. Lower values darken the screen display.

The optimal Gamma value lies between 1.2 and 2.0

The "neutral" value for PhotoImpact lies at 1.8. Normally, the optimal Gamma value should lie between 1.2 and 2.0. Other values are unusual. If you need another value, you might have set the brightness for the monitor incorrectly.

More advanced calibration options

More expensive image editing programs like Adobe Photoshop often offer more advanced options for calibrating the monitor display.

1 Photoshop comes with a calibration tool you can access through the Control Panel.

7. Everything in tune: Calibrating your devices

2 You can operate the program with the help of a Wizard or through the illustrated dialog window.

3 The *View Single Gamma Only* option also removes colorcasts. If the option is disabled ...

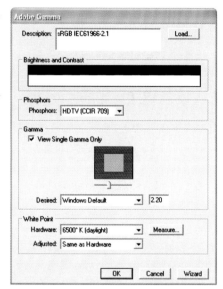

4 ... you can regulate each color channel individually.

5 The most practical thing about this calibration tool is that the settings are in effect outside of Photoshop as well.

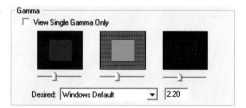

Back to the page – Printing out scans

After you have completed all steps from scanning to formatting the printer, you have only one more step to complete: the actual printing. After all, you don't want to stop at admiring your work on the screen. For this reason, you learn in this chapter the things to consider when you print.

Printing a video label

For our example, we have chosen to create a video label in PhotoDeluxe. In Photo-Deluxe, you can find a multitude of templates in different categories under *Cards & More*.

1 Switch to *Cards & More*. Choose the *Media Labels* entry from the *Labels & Frames* menu.

2 In the first step, select *Choose Media Label*.

3 You have a choice of different designs from the template catalog. Double-click the illustrated entry.

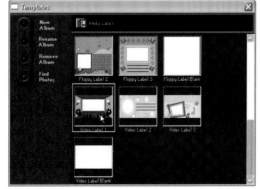

8. Back to the page – Printing out scans

Scaleable templates

All PhotoDeluxe templates are in the EPS file format. This format allows you to scale the size of the image you are using without any loss in quality.

4 The selected video label is now opened in a separate window.

5 To insert your own picture in the empty area, go to the second step and select *Open File*.

6 The selected picture is placed inside a frame in the empty area.

7 Drag the picture so that it fills the entire area. That's it. Now you can save the document.

Using the print preview

Most programs have a print preview in which you can check the result before you print it out.

1 From the *Print* menu, select the option *Print Multiple on a Page*. This option allows you to print several labels on the same page and save time and paper.

2 You can find out how it all looks in the print preview, which opens after you select the command.

There you can view the currently selected paper format. Click the *Change* button to change the label type.

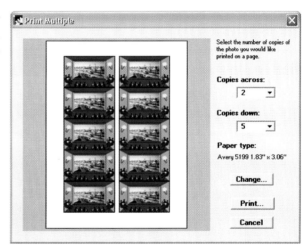

Printer selection

Now you must adjust the default factory settings. First, let PhotoDeluxe know which printer to use for printing.

8. Back to the page - Printing out scans

1 Click *Print.* A standard Windows dialog window opens in which you can select the desired printer (in the illustration, it's an Epson printer).

2 Open the next dialog window by clicking *Setup.* You probably already know this dialog window from other applications.

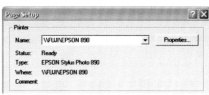

3 Click *Properties* ...

4 ... to change the printer settings.

The available setting options might vary widely from printer to printer. In the illustration, you can see the properties for our printer.

Selecting the right settings

Let's take a look at the settings to which you should pay most attention. The Epson Stylus Photo printer is used as an example, but other printer drivers might have different options.

1 In the *Ink* area, determine whether you want to print out in color or black-and-white. For test prints, select *Black* to save ink.

2 Choose the *Automatic* function in the *Mode* area to let the printer driver calculate the best settings.

Always use the right paper

When you print with an inkjet printer, the paper used makes a lot of difference. For mass printouts, you can of course use normal photocopy paper because it's the cheapest.

This paper soaks up the ink rather badly, however. This leads to the printed dots flowing into one another, which makes the picture darker and less brilliant.

If you want to create the perfect printout, you should use another kind of paper. Different papers are available for inkjet printers; they are rather expensive, however.

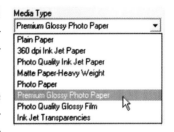

These papers have a smooth surface that keeps the ink from being absorbed. This results in luminous colors. If you are using such glossy paper, select the corresponding option from the list box. The printer driver automatically sets the correct resolution values for every paper type.

A special paper collection

Do you use specialty papers rather often but don't want to spend too much on them? Then you should take a look at DATA BECKER's paper collection. Because all of these papers are well-priced, it's worth giving them a try. For more information on the collection, go to DATA BECKER's home page at *http://www.databecker.com*

The right paper format

In the *Paper* tab, set the size of the paper you want to use. As you might already know from other programs, the *Media Type* list box contains a few standard formats. In addition, you can determine here how many copies of the document you want.

8. Back to the page – Printing out scans

The *Maximal* option, also located on this tab, is also interesting. You need to enable this option if you want the paper to be printed all the way to the edge.

In addition, you can enter the number of copies here as well.

And out it comes: Starting the printing process

After having made all the necessary setting adjustments, you can now start the actual printing process.

1 To start the printing process in PhotoDeluxe, close the dialog windows and click *OK*.

2 The data is then sent to the printer.

3 If everything went as planned, you can now admire a great printout.

What should you do if the printout is bad?

What if everything didn't go as planned? Perhaps your printout is too dark or it has a colorcast. Let's see what you can do to correct that.

At this point, you must basically rely on the printer driver; if it doesn't offer you any options, then you have to use the functions in the image-editing program. In our example, we can make changes in the printer driver, so we don't need to change the actual image data.

1 To make changes, you must go through the already described steps until you find the *Advanced* button; click it. The setting options open in a separate dialog window. Here, you can adjust how intense the colors should be printed.

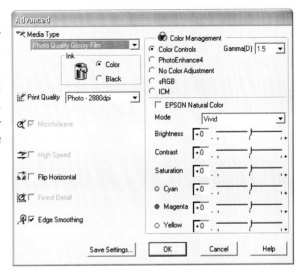

2 If you are printing a photograph, choose between *Photo-realistic* and *Vivid*.

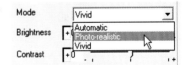

3 In the *Print Quality* list box, you can change the resolution of the printout. For test prints, you can set a lower value; for the final printout, use the highest possible value.

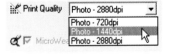

Always test-print at low resolution

If you want to print out as a test only, it is worth printing at low resolution, for the printing goes much faster, and you save ink.

4 In the Gamma field, you can change the brightness of the midtones: the lower the Gamma value, the lighter the result is. A value of 1.5 is usually quite good.

Adjusting the color and brightness

On the bottom right, you can find options for adjusting the color as well as the contrast and brightness of the printout. All the important settings are there if your printout is too dark or too light, or if it has a colorcast.

1 In the first area, you can change the brightness, contrast, and saturation. If the colors in your printout are too pale, for instance, you can use the saturation slider to make the colors more intense.

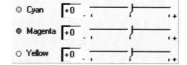

Note

Always change contrast and brightness in larger steps

If you want to change the contrast or the brightness, make large changes from the beginning. Try out values that are 10 to 15% higher or lower than the original. If you make smaller changes, you can have a hard time seeing a difference between the printouts.

---

2 Use the three-color sliders to remove colorcasts. If you raise the cyan value, for instance, the printout is bluer.

Note

Color corrections necessitate a few trials

When making color corrections, you must more than likely give it a few tries. It takes some practice to remove colorcasts. The entire task is made even more difficult because printers don't work with the RGB color system but with the CMYK system. You already met the two color systems in the third chapter of this book.

No options need to be changed!

With the Epson printer, you have the opportunity to adjust the printer over the settings for the printer driver, but what should you do if you're using a printer whose driver doesn't have any setting options?

You need to fall back on the functions in your image-editing program.

Changing the image data

In this case, you must be careful. When you change the settings for the printer driver, you don't change the actual picture; the changes only affect the printout.

It's a different story, however, when you fall back on the functions in your image-editing program. In this case, you change the image properties permanently.

In PhotoDeluxe, the options for correcting the image are located under *Adjust Quality*, illustrated here. The functions are similar to those in most image-editing programs.

Changing the brightness and contrast

To change the brightness or contrast of the image, click Brightness/Contrast. Adjust the settings in the dialog window that opens and which is illustrated

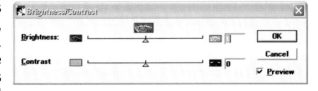

here. If the *Preview* option is enabled, check the result in the original image on the spot.

Changing the color balance

If your image has a colorcast, you need to use the *Fix Color* option.

8. Back to the page – Printing out scans

1 First, switch to the *Variations* tab.

2 In a large dialog window, you can comfortably remove colorcasts by clicking the preview images.

You might click the same field more than once. When you have achieved the desired result, close the dialog window by clicking *OK*.

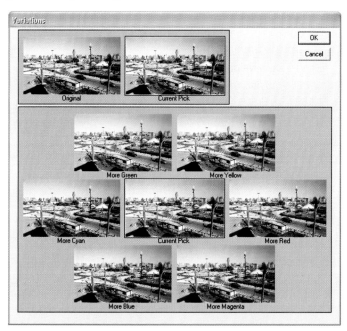

Changing the tone and saturation

The *Adjust Quality* menu also has a function for changing the saturation. In addition, you can change the hue here.

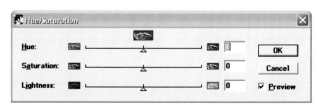

138

Resizing the image

Have you changed your mind? Do you want to turn the little card into a poster or vice versa? Then you must adjust the size of the image. Reaching the resizing option is a little complicated: in the navigation bar at the bottom, click the *Advanced Menus* option.

1 Once you do this, several additional entries appear in the menu bar. The Photoshop experts can find a number of well-known functions here, but let's not confuse the newbies.

A powerful program

Once you have gotten used to PhotoDeluxe, you should take a look at the advanced menus. There, you can find many interesting functions that reveal the parentage of PhotoDeluxe: Photoshop, the "cousin" of PhotoDeluxe and standard tool of image editing professionals.

2 Go to *Size/Photo Size*, to open the illustrated dialog window.

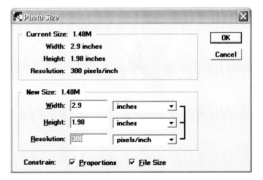

3 Enter the new measurements of the picture in the text entry fields, but make sure that the *File Size* option is disabled. Otherwise, only the resolution changes and the file size remains the same.

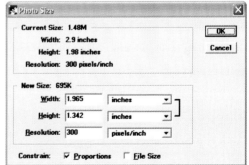

Don't feel like typing? – OCR

In this final chapter, you encounter one more area of use for your scanner: OCR. The abbreviation stands for **O**ptical **C**haracter **R**ecognition.

Behind the name hides an interesting technology. OCR programs translate scanned pixel images into editable text. The OCR program thus makes it possible to edit already printed text in your text editing program without your having to retype it, saving you time.

What can OCR software do?

Most scanners come with light-version OCR programs. These versions usually offer only a fraction of the functions available with the full version. Some scanners even come with limited-function programs that only work for a certain time period.

In this chapter, you try out different programs offering different possibilities. Cuneiform is shareware you can download from *http://www.ocr.com*.

OCR – Not always a success

In general, don't expect too much from the functionality of these programs. The recognition rate depends on the original. Flowery writing is rarely recognized, for instance. In addition, you have to first expand the existing dictionaries. For this reason, the first few times you use such a program, check the results more thoroughly.

Text recognition with Presto! OCR

Our scanner came with the OCR program Presto! OCR, so use this program for your first test. You can decide whether the text to be recognized is already scanned, or whether to scan it during the recognition process.

1 Start the Epson Smart Panel. From here, you can start many utilities, including Scan to OCR.

2 The program opens in a preview area, in which you can determine the area you want to scan. As an alternative, you can open the TWAIN module from here.

Enable the *Grayscale* option (it makes no sense to scan text in color).

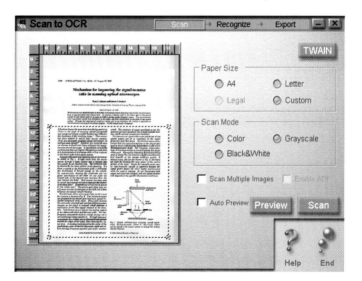

9. Don't feel like typing? – OCR

3 After the scan, a dialog window opens in which you can enter the language you want to use and the recognition module.

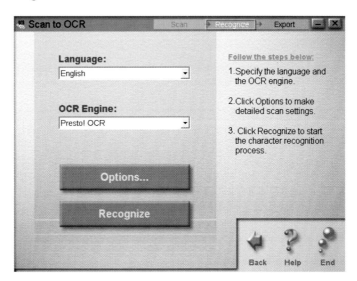

4 Now you need to determine whether you want to save the result as a text file ...

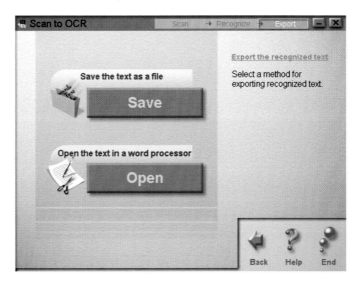

... or whether you want to open it in a text-editing program.

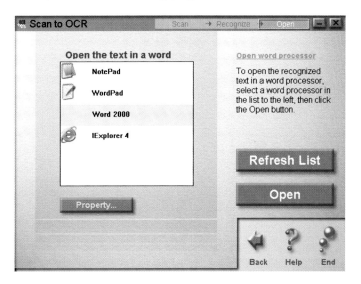

5 The automatic recognition is now started.

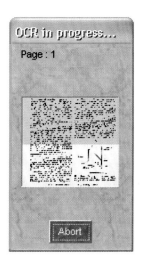

6 You can also use a program such as OmniPage Pro independently of the OCR software included. The advantage to doing so is that you can now control the result.

This way, you can correct the highlighted words (about which the program was in doubt), for instance.

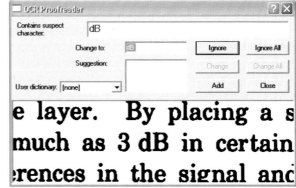

Text recognition with Cuneiform

In the next example, you use Cuneiform version 3.1.

1 Start the program. Although the program interface is not attractive, it is easy to understand and well designed.

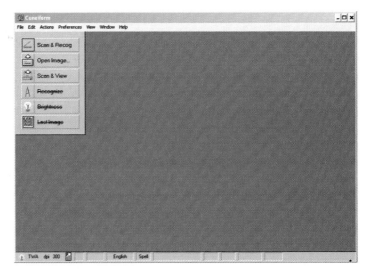

2 Before you scan the document, choose the verification language. To do so, go to *Actions/Set Language*.

3 If you have downloaded the correct version from the Internet, you can find *English* in the list box.

4 Now start the scanning and recognition process by clicking *Scan & Recog*.

5 The already familiar TWAIN module window opens.

6 It is important to enable the *Line Art* option during recognition; this way, the image is scanned only in black and white.

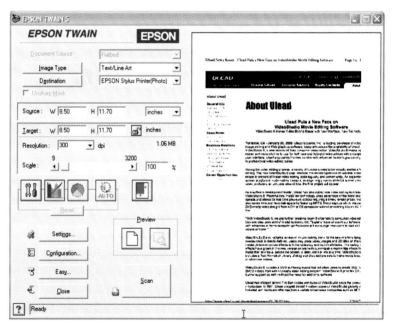

7 You already know how to select the right image area. Drag the frame in the preview image to the desired size.

Avoid additional work by selecting the right area

Be careful not to select any superfluous areas, because Cuneiform tries to translate all letters. For graphic elements, you might therefore obtain some pretty weird recognition results. Then, you must delete many superfluous letters. You can avoid the additional work by selecting the right area.

9. Don't feel like typing? – OCR

After the scanning is complete, two windows open in Cuneiform: one for the recognized text and one for the scanned image (see the next illustration).

In the window of the recognized text, all words that the program couldn't recognize or which were not in the dictionary are highlighted in green.

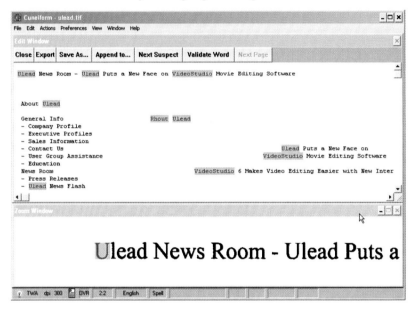

Checking the OCR results

Now you must check the result and correct any words that were recognized incorrectly.

1 Cuneiform goes to the first highlighted word. At the same time, the word's position is highlighted in the scanned image.

In our example, the program interpreted the letter combination "Ab" as "Rh". Correct the word in the upper window.

2 After the correction, click *Validate Word* or press Ctrl+W.

> **Validate Word**

This makes the highlighting disappear. If the word is not in the dictionary, it is now added to it.

Adding words to the dictionary

If a highlighted word is actually correct, press Ctrl+W to add the unknown word to the dictionary. The highlighting then disappears from all instances of the word in the text.

3 To get to the next highlighted word, either click *Next Suspect* or press Tab.

> **Next Suspect**

Overwrite mode

Cuneiform automatically works in overwrite mode. This means that when you type in a letter, the letter that was previously located at that position is automatically deleted. To insert a letter, you must first press Insert.

4 Edit the text piece by piece until you have removed all highlighting from the text.

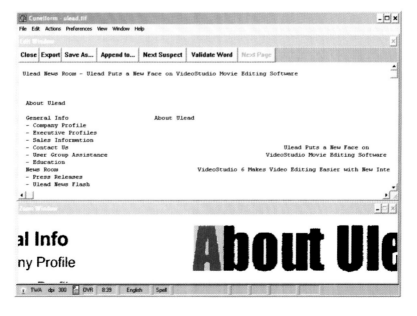

Saving recognized text

Once you have checked the text, save it as its own text file.

1 To do so, click *Save As.*

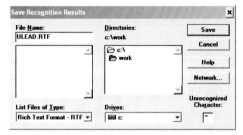

2 Different text formats are available in which to save your document. If you want to save the formatting as well, use the RTF file format.

3 This is the text as it appears in Word.

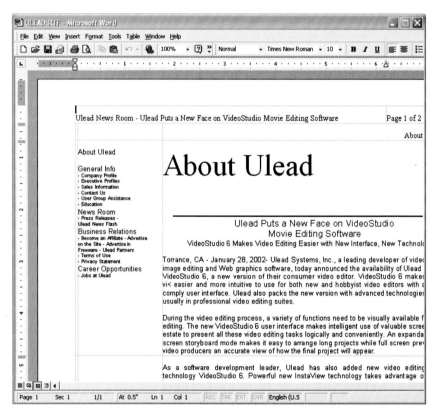

The formatting is preserved

Cuneiform has preserved most of the formatting: italicized text appears italicized, and bold text appears bold.

Saving the dictionary

Now close the window. If you want to save the image, go to *File/Save Image*. If you don't want to validate unknown words again next time, save the dictionary:

1 If you close the document by clicking *Close* ...

2 ... this window is automatically opened. It contains all the unknown words Cuneiform found during the recognition process.

Make sure all the entries are correct. If not, click the word you need to correct. You can then change it or delete it using the buttons underneath the list.

Then, click *Dict*.

3 The dictionaries are saved with the file ending USV.

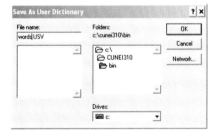

Changing certain sections

Another mode is available in Cuneiform, which is quickly introduced here.

9. Don't feel like typing? – OCR

1 In the menu bar, go to *Preferences/Manual Layout*. A checkmark in front of the entry shows which function is enabled.

2 After you call up *Scan & Recog*, the window illustrated here opens.

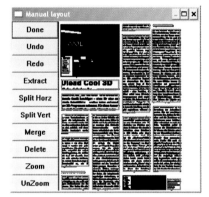

Here, all sections in which Cuneiform has recognized text are marked.

3 If you can see any sections that you want to exclude from the text recognition, click the corresponding frame and then click *Delete*.

4 In the example, you don't need any of the sections containing the title of the book.

Enlarged view

If you can't see parts of the picture well, use the *Zoom* option to enlarge the preview image.

5 Delete all superfluous sections one by one. On the left, you can see the selected text blocks.

Adding sections

If a section containing text is not selected, click *Extract*; then draw a frame around the section in the preview image.

6 Click *Done* to start the scanning process.   Done

7 The rest of the process is identical to the one previously described.

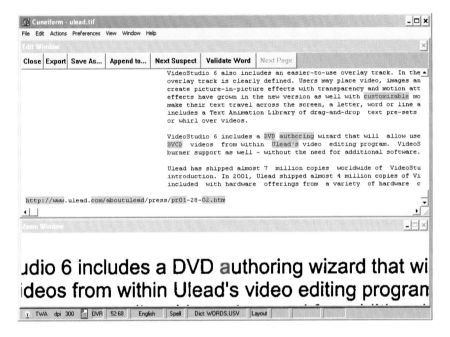

Scanning a signature

Sometimes, having your signature in digital form can be practical. For this reason, let's look at how you can save your digital signature with Paint Shop Pro.

1 Simply sign your name on an empty piece of paper using a pen with a broad tip or a marker.

2 Go to *Import/TWAIN/Select Source* to call up the correct TWAIN driver.

9. Don't feel like typing? – OCR

3 Select the desired scanner from the dialog window.

4 Go to *Import/TWAIN/Acquire* to start the scanning process.

5 This starts the TWAIN module. First, scan a preview as usual.

6 You could scan a black-and-white copy directly from the TWAIN driver, but take another route.

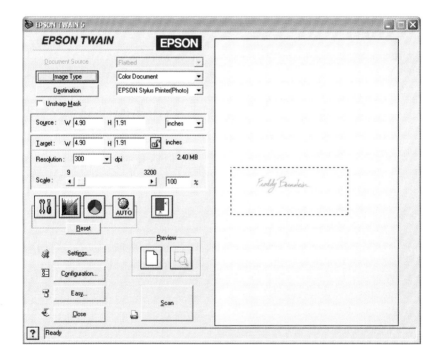

Click *Scan* in the TWAIN driver to start the scanning process.

7 The scanned picture is now imported into the editing area.

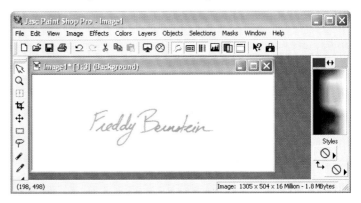

Cropping and preparing the signature

After you have scanned the signature, you must prepare it. For instance, you should crop any superfluous margins.

1 To do so, select the *Cropping* tool from the toolbar.

2 Drag open a frame around the area you want to crop.

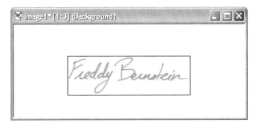

3 After you confirm your selection, the areas outside of the frame are cut off. To remove them, double-click inside the frame.

4 If you want the signature to be black, go to *Colors/ Grey Scale*.

5 In addition, increase the contrast until the background is entirely white (select *Colors/Adjust/Brightness/Contrast* for this). Through the heightened contrast, the signature also seems of a more saturated black.

On the left, notice the settings used for the example.

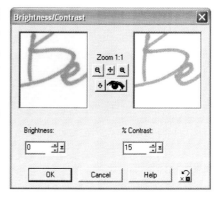

6 Finally, save the result by going to *File/Save As*. You can use the BMP format, for instance.

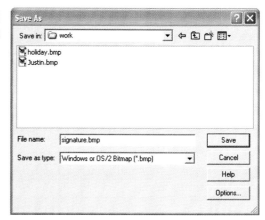

Index

155

Index

Notes

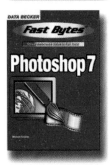